THE ISLE OF WIGHT

A SHELL GUIDE

SHELL GUIDES

edited by JOHN BETJEMAN AND JOHN PIPER

★

DORSET
Michael Pitt-Rivers

CORNWALL
John Betjeman

RUTLAND
W. G. Hoskins

SUFFOLK
Norman Scarfe

MID-WALES
BRECON, RADNOR and MONTGOMERY
David Verey

SOUTH-WEST WALES
PEMBROKESHIRE and CARMARTHENSHIRE
Vyvyan Rees

NORFOLK
Wilhelmine Harrod and the Rev. C. L. S. Linnell

SHROPSHIRE
John Piper and John Betjeman

THE WEST COAST OF SCOTLAND
Stephen Bone

GLOUCESTERSHIRE
Anthony West and David Verey

OXFORDSHIRE
John Piper

DEVON
Brian Watson

NORTHUMBERLAND
Thomas Sharp

HEREFORDSHIRE
David Verey

WILTSHIRE
David Verey

WORCESTERSHIRE
James Lees-Milne

PILOT TO THE SOUTH COAST HARBOURS
K. Adlard Coles

ALUM BAY: a Victorian sand picture made from the coloured sands of the cliffs and sold as a souvenir

THE
ISLE OF WIGHT

by
PENNETHORNE HUGHES

FABER AND FABER LIMITED
24 RUSSELL SQUARE LONDON

First published in mcmlxvii
by Faber and Faber Limited
24 Russell Square London WC1
Printed in Great Britain by
W. S. Cowell Ltd, Ipswich
All rights reserved

ILLUSTRATIONS

INTRODUCTION

To those born there, and to thousands of others, the Isle of Wight is simply "The Island". It is an affectionate and almost proprietary term. "Insular" tends to mean exclusive, and Wight has been exclusive in two ways: something apart and self-contained, and something fashionable. New communications have diminished both. The Island is now accessible and "overners" (as people from the mainland are known) are no longer strange intruders into a private world. Islanders no longer make their wills, as a matter of course, before visiting the mainland, which they did in the 17th century. Nor are the pleasures of the Island confined to those who can afford expensive annual holidays, with yachting part of the social season enjoyed only by an élite. The precariously placed but comparatively uneventful island which suddenly blossomed with the social revolution of the Victorian era into a garden resort for the upper classes is now part of the pattern of the democratic holiday industry. From this thousands benefit. For those who regret the past, however, it still exists. There are the antiquities of any English countryside, and built upon them the Regency, Victorian and Edwardian evidences we are now beginning to enjoy. The holiday edge – the east coast conurbation – has modern entertainment along its sheltered sands. But the interior has the old Wight of the villages, Ventnor and Ryde have their marine villas climbing with period charm, and the downs, though they prickle with transmitter masts, as yet remain. Although intruded and overrun in the summer, the Island is still pleasant to live in, and pleasant to visit.

COWES: The Royal Yacht Squadron

DESCRIPTION

Topography The Isle of Wight was once part of the mainland, and the Solent was a river. There are legends of a road crossing to Hampshire in as late as Roman times, although this remains antiquarian conjecture. Now the Solent is some five miles wide, an historic navigational channel, with the freak bonus of double high tides which have made Southampton the port it is, and also operate at the three harbours of Yarmouth, Cowes and Newport.

The island is small: twenty-three miles from east to west, and thirteen from north to south, at its widest points. The coast is sixty miles round, and the area 155 square miles, that is, some 94,000 acres, approximately one acre to each permanent inhabitant. (The population at least doubles during the summer season.) Inside this area there is an astonishing variety of scenery. It is a microcosm, in which heights become mountains, and valleys gorges. The coastline is wild and dangerous, luxuriant and tropical, or gentle and conventional. All this has been overwritten, first by the romantic guide books of the era of the early Victorian development, and today by the giddy superlatives of holiday publicists. There can therefore be a sense of deflation in finding everything so small, confined and accessible – it is like seeing a number of stock photographs thrown down almost on top of each other on a pretty tablecloth. This sense of overcrowded incident, each itself a little less than was promised, usually disappears, however, and the charm of the Island lies in the fact that every few miles brings a new contrast.

Through the middle of the Island, from Bembridge in the east to the Needles in the west, lies a range of chalk hills, the downs, which are its dominating feature. Another range runs along the south coast from St Catherine's to near Shanklin. On the north the land slopes down in wooded folds to the sea, but at the western end the cliffs are precipitous, with many caves. Along the south landslips throughout history have caused for most of the way a double coastline, with high cliffs inland and below a shelf of debris which in the sheltered belt of the Undercliff proper (see pp. 56, 59) is covered with exotic foliage where myrtles and other unusual plants grow vigorously in the open air, in sub-tropical extravagance. Along the south, too, are the sharp indentations of the chines, which are clefts in the solid rock. All round the coast are bays, each with its own characteristics – Alum Bay and its coloured sands, Freshwater Bay with its rocks, Chale with its wrecks, or Sandown with its visitors. All this is best recognized from the sea.

From north to south the river Medina bisects the Island. It rises at the base of St Catherine's Down and flows northward to Cowes. Apart from this, although there are many brooks and rivulets, the only real rivers are confusingly both called Yar. The Western Yar begins only a few hundred yards from the English Channel at Freshwater Bay, and flows north to join the Solent at Yarmouth. The Eastern Yar winds from the south-east coast up to Bembridge. There are streams running into the deep creeks of Newtown and Wootton. Parkhurst, or what is left of it, is the only real forest.

The Medina serves descriptively to name the two halves of the Island, quite separate in character, West Medina and East Medina. "Back of the Wight" describes the southern part of the Island west of the Undercliff. It hardly does so, however, to the geologist with his specialized interest. But few tourists today take with them, as did their grandfathers, a geological hammer and a copy of William Smith's *Strata Identified by Organised Fossils*. It should be noted, however, that the Island does provide quite exceptionally accessible evidence of stratification, and is prolific of fossils. The story is in the Museum of Isle of Wight Geology at Sandown. But captive in souvenirs, or carelessly washed along the beaches, shells and the preserved bric-à-brac of nature's prehistory exist for any child to wonder at.

There are many wildflowers, migratory birds, adders, and other natural curiosities. There are no badgers or polecats, and foxes did not exist until the sportsmen imported them from the mainland in the 19th century. Game fowl is plentiful, and often met with even on the main roads.

The buildings of the Island are appropriate rather than remarkable, and attract more from their setting than from any magnificence. The old churches – ten are mentioned in Domesday – have their points for the ecclesiologist, and are of course the working centres of interest for the social historian. Because of the wave of interest in the romantic and antiquarian which excited the Victorian visitor, the older guide-books faithfully date each pillar and describe each piscina. Visitors still flock to these churches, partly from guidebook momentum, and very pretty some of them are – Shalfleet, Godshill, St Lawrence and Carisbrooke. Most of them have excellent descriptive leaflets. But although they have the charm of all old village churches, and fine detail, they are much the same architectural re-paints as others in Hampshire or in Dorset – Norman bits, Middle-English walls, Tudor extensions and Victorian-Perpendicular restorations. It is the specialist on Victorian church architecture who will find the Island a quarry, and enjoy Gilbert Scott's All Saints at Ryde, Temple Moore's The Good Shepherd at Lake, and the numerous other churches run up to meet the growing and mainly wealthy congregations of the developing resorts. Erected of alien materials, by an alien community, Quarr Abbey stands as a separate modern ecclesiastical building, sharp in

Chalk cliffs, near THE NEEDLES

contrast to the weathering of the old Island churches, and vivid amongst the greyness of those of the great Victorians.

In domestic architecture the Island has no Longleat or Blenheim. There are satisfying gentlemen's country seats of the eighteenth century, but the only major Palladian building of the Island, Appuldurcombe, is a shell. On the other hand there are any number of excellent Tudor and Jacobean manor houses, of which a number are noticed in detail in the gazetteer. Many can be visited, but a high proportion, compared with most parts of the mainland, remain in private hands. In several villages, and notably at Arreton and Kingston, there is the classic grouping of church, manor and manor-farm. Dotted all along the cliffs, and sometimes perched inland, are Regency and early Victorian villas. Many, and amongst them the more exotic examples of the marine cottage ornée, as shown in the old prints, have disappeared. Enough remains to delight the connoisseur. Many of the crenellated Gothic revival castles have disappeared as well, the last to go being John Nash's splendid nonsense of East Cowes Castle, now a housing estate. Of the great ones only Wyatt's Norris Castle remains, looking out over the Solent. Nearby,

and trying to think of the water as the Bay of Naples, is Prince Albert's adapted Italianate Osborne House, with down the road, over-looking the Medina, the equally improbable royal church at Whippingham.

Outstanding public buildings are Carisbrooke Castle, those of the Tudor forts which still remain, Victorian barracks, Ryde Pier, and the administrative nexus round the jail at Parkhurst.

The cottages and farms are many of them pretty: stone, good thatch or tile, of any period from the late middle ages to Edwardian. Later they are brick, sometimes patterned and very ugly, and become villas. And bungalows. And chalets, with built-in obsolescence.

There remain the towns. Yarmouth and Newport have some old buildings, and the character of continuity. The rest are resorts, some of them running into each other, like Shanklin, Lake and Sandown. Before long no doubt the whole coastline will, apart from areas artificially preserved as breathing spaces, be a continuous rash of contemporary one-storey buildings for recreation or retirement, variegated by concrete. This is not yet so, and whilst the watering places retain their individ-uality, the pendulum of taste means that their marine rows and crescents, of the post 1830 boom, are what many people will most ad-mire. They may well do so. Ventnor, Ryde – even Freshwater and the others – have delight-ful sea-side terraces, and the period balconies and ornate pilasters, the stucco fronts and external verandahs climb up delightfully enough amongst the conifers, above the lawns and awnings of the sea-fronts. They are the local expression of the great burst of building development and improvement that took place all over England after 1837. But whilst Plymouth was built by Foulston, Cheltenham by Papworth, Hastings and Brighton by Decimus Burton, and Newcastle

BEMBRIDGE: North Wells

ST CATHERINE'S POINT, with the lighthouse

by Dobson, no great builder designed the towns of the Isle of Wight. Nash came to retire here as a gentleman, not to practise as a developer. The speculators were little men, who built the "genteel residences" and profit-able boarding-houses. The "men of taste" deplored what was being done. One wrote of Ryde, in 1838, "The houses more resemble a slice of second-rate fashionable London, stuck on the side of the Island, than anything which one would be prepared to meet with."

13

VENTNOR: Houses on the sea front

Brannon, whose pictures of "Vectis scenery" of 1862 did so much to popularize the natural beauties of the Island, lamented both the excesses of the Gothic style and the depraved eighteenth-century façades of the boarding-houses. Now we swallow them all, with the brand description "Regency", and are delighted.

Delightful they frequently are. So, to another taste, are many of the new buildings. And all can be grateful that the Island not only avoided the devastation of the first industrial revolution but is showing architectural restraint in welcoming the new. Factories are neat, and there are no skyscrapers, as yet.

That the Island still has a Governor is special but history. That it is also a county in its own right is special and contemporary. For long it was part of Hampshire. It gained administrative independence in 1890. It has a pride, and in spite of the holiday industry is not grasping or servile. The Island's propaganda is still largely justified. There is much besides a palace, a prison, a castle, a yachting centre and all those side-shows where once there were only wrecks and sea-shells.

HISTORICAL NOTE

"Fortunate is the country that has no history" – at all events in headlines. The Isle of Wight has been pretty lucky. Great naval battles were fought off its coasts, it endured Danish and French invading parties, and did not relish a Scottish regiment or English soldiers who were respectively billeted in it in the 17th and 20th centuries. But it did not see fighting in the Wars of the Roses, or during the Civil Wars. In the last war it was bombed but nowhere devastated. Its social pattern has been that of rural southern England, with its industries those of fishing and agriculture, varied by quarrying, shipbuilding, lace manufacture and smuggling. Strategically vital, it remained socially a backwater until the time of our grandfathers.

Flint implements, middens, pottery and tumuli suggest a general culture during the Bronze Age comparable to Dorset and Hampshire, although in no way as intense or important as that of Wiltshire. The Island slipped uneventfully into the Iron Age, and into chronicle when occupied by the Romans, under Vespasian, in AD 43. They called it Vectis, a Latinization of a Celtic Ynys-yr-Wyth, which became more easily the Saxon Weet, or Wight. Romantic attempts to connect Vectis with the Ictis mentioned by the Greek Diodorus as a centre of the Phoenician tin-trade are now reluctantly discountenanced, and most historians have settled for St Michael's Mount in Cornwall. But both for strategic reasons and because of its situation, climate, and indeed oysters, Vectis must have been an acceptable station for the Romans, and the villas at Brading and elsewhere show late and sophisticated occupation. But Christianity (says the venerable and inevitable Bede) came late: the Isle of Wight was the last corner of Britain to be converted. It then became part of the diocese of Winchester for some twelve hundred years, until 1927, when the new see of Portsmouth was created.

After the departure of the Romans the usual pall of confusion descends, but the Island was colonized by Jutes and then by Saxons, although Cerdic the West-Saxon, who captured Carisbrooke and so the Island in AD 530, had Celtic affinities. The place-names of the Island are almost all Saxon. The Danes raided the Island and had a base there. It was overrun by the Northmen from the North and then the Northmen from France, the Normans. When William I conquered England (or, as he always claimed, entered into his inheritance) the Isle of Wight, like the Channel Islands, was not made part of the English realm. It retained its separate identity, more or less, for another 200 years, and it always seems strange that it has not made more of the fact. After Hastings, William gave it to be ruled by his cousin William Fitz-Osborne, who was also made Earl of Hereford and Seneschal and Marshall of Normandy and England. Fitz-Osborne's successor chose the wrong side in the dynastic upsets after William's death, and Henry I granted the Island to Richard de Redvers, Earl of Devon. It descended to a William de Redvers, better known as William de Vernon, in 1184. He was a great feudal lord of the Island, but even grander state was maintained by his descendant Isabella, Countess of Albemarle, Countess of Devon and Lady of the Isle of Wight, who lived at Carisbrooke in almost regal splendour, long remembered. On her death-bed she was forced – some historians think cheated – into selling the Island to Edward I for a ridiculously small sum. It was only then, in 1293, that the Isle of Wight finally became part of the realm of England.

The reasons for the purchase were strategic. There in the narrow seas the Island was as vital in the French wars as the Cinque Ports farther along the English coast. Like them it was subject to frequent French raids, of which the most important was one in 1377, when a landing party burned Yarmouth, Newport and Newtown. The French monks from Lyra in Normandy were expelled, as a potential fifth column.

With Henry VIII came the dissolution of the monasteries altogether, and Quarr Abbey was sold to a Southampton firm who traded back many of the stones to help build the new castles created to guard the Solent, at Yarmouth, Cowes and Sandown. The Captains of the Island remobilized the local defence forces, and Queen Elizabeth had new outer walls made for Carisbrooke. Much of Parkhurst Forest was felled to provide ships for the royal navies, often built in the Cowes shipyards. Inside the Island new Tudor gentry like the Worsleys began to build their manor houses, and to mix with the old Island families like the Oglanders, who had been settled at the time of the Norman Conquest. The Civil Wars left the Island largely undisturbed, and indeed it became something of a funk-hole for rich refugees from the mainland. The price of land rocketed. The gentry were many of them royalist, but the Island was Parliamentarian, and there was never any suggestion of a popular effort to rescue King Charles during his captivity at Carisbrooke. (There is a note about this on p. 17). The sheep grazed undisturbed on the downs, new Jacobean manors were built in the valleys, and the smuggling continued along the coasts.

So it did throughout the 18th century without any major external forces operating to make life different from that on the mainland. The Island was still sometimes cut off for days at a time, when there was fog in the Solent. With the turn of the century came a quickening interest. Romantic scenery was becoming fashionable, country retreats were in vogue, little Strawberry Hills were being planted. The great demagogue John Wilkes had built his "villakins" at Sandown in 1778, and Garrick and other fashionable figures had been visitors. George Morland was painting rural landscapes, and living the low life amongst the smugglers and fishermen of the Island. The crowds were to follow.

The great Victorian discovery of the Isle of Wight as a holiday centre was due in part to the social revolution created by a rich middle class. Professional men and wealthy manufacturers after the Napoleonic wars could afford to travel, if hardly to take their swelling families on the Grand Tour. This meant the rise of the English watering places: not now so much Bath and Brighton, but Cheltenham, Folkestone and even, adventurously, in the West Country. For many the Isle of Wight was ideal. It was an island, but now accessible, and the first steam packet ran between Ryde and Portsmouth in 1826. It was healthy, and its remarkable climate was medically and publicly endorsed by Sir James Clark in 1829. It was "romantic", and the pursuit of the picturesque was in vogue: the Island's contrasting hills and cliffs became mountains and lowering precipices. Above all, the place was charming, and for children a Paradise.

When Queen Victoria bought the Osborne estate in 1845, and Tennyson moved to Farringford, the Island entered its great days. Already, and since Regency times, Cowes and Ryde were the centres of yachting. Now came the poets, the politicians and above all the middle classes, with their interest in the scenic and antiquarian. The day trippers followed. Still the old Island families lived on, as some still do, and agriculture and the sea remained basic industries. But new buildings went up for the new visitors and the retired people: first the cottages ornées and the crenellated castles, then the rows of boarding houses and

"Cheerful Spring" A painting of inland Wight by G. F. Watts

villas; and later the bandstands. Now, rather less hideous than on most parts of the south coast, there erupt bungalows, chalets, and the unequivocal architecture of light industry.

A succession of Governors and Captains, many of them men of note in other spheres, have held titular authority. The governorship has been honorary since 1841, with nothing but formal duties to perform. But there has been a recent continuity of tenure. Prince Henry of Battenberg was appointed Governor in 1889, and was succeeded by his widow, Princess Beatrice, who died in 1944. Their son, Lord Mountbatten of Burma, was installed in this ancient office on 26th July 1965.

CHARLES I AT CARISBROOKE

A king in captivity is romantic. A Stuart in captivity had a special poignancy for Queen Victoria, who was proud of her Scottish connection. The two circumstances have made Charles I's imprisonment at Carisbrooke a peak in the Island's history, although it in fact gratefully escaped the fighting and most of the upheaval of the Civil Wars. On 3rd June 1647, Charles, defeated in the field, was seized and held at Hampton Court Palace, a pawn between the army and Parliament. Extremists threatened his life. His followers felt that the newly appointed Governor of the Isle of Wight, which was anyhow part of the way to France, might be sympathetic, as he was a nephew of the King's Chaplain. But Colonel Robert Hammond had seen distinguished service with the Parliamentarians, and was also connected by marriage to Oliver Cromwell. He was vague to the king's messengers, but they unwisely thought he could be relied on, and the king crossed the Solent secretly, one night in November, and went into residence at Carisbrooke. At first he was treated with respect, and allowed to travel about the Island, hunt in Parkhurst Forest, and take dinner with Sir John Oglander and the gentry of the Island. But he continued to negotiate secretly with the Scots, signing a treaty by which they would invade England and restore him to the throne. There was an abortive rising on his behalf on the mainland. Hammond now received orders to hold him a close prisoner, and this was done, his only recreation being to play on the new bowling green made on the site of the old tilt yard. He made two dramatic attempts to escape. On March 20th 1648 the guard was to be drugged and the King to escape through a window of the Great Chamber. He had omitted to establish that he could get more than his head between the bar and the mullion, stuck half way, and the attempt ignominiously failed. There was consternation and further plotting and signalling up and down the valley. Henry Firebrace, the follower who had organized the first attempt, acquired files and acid to cut through the bars of the room to which Charles had now been moved behind the curtain wall itself. This second attempt was planned for May 28th, and an escape route was planned and ready. At the last moment it was betrayed. Charles stayed on at Carisbrooke until September 6th, when he was moved on parole to Newport for the negotiations with Parliament which ended in the abortive Treaty of Newport. On November 30th he was escorted from the Island back to the mainland and his eventual execution.

In August 1649 two of the king's children were brought to Carisbrooke: Henry, Duke of Gloucester, aged ten, whom Cromwell thought it would be best "to bind to a trade", but who was eventually released, and the rather pathetic Princess Elizabeth, a weak child of thirteen, who took a chill and died on September 8th 1650. She is buried at Newport. This brief episode was all. The Island obeys, almost extravagantly, the royal injunction from the scaffold, "Remember".

> ## The Five Guidebook Wonders
>
> Needles you cannot thread,
> Cowes you cannot milk,
> Freshwater you cannot drink,
> Newport you cannot bottle,
> Ryde where you can walk.

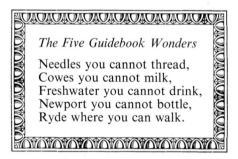

YARMOUTH: The statue in the Church of Sir Robert Holmes, Governor of the Isle of Wight 1667–1692. The head and the body are by different sculptors

GAZETTEER

The number after the place name refers to the square on the map where the place is to be found.

Alverstone Mill [14]. A pretty inland village 2½ miles west of Sandown. It is much visited, and the cottages, some stone and thatched, do teas on the lawn. There is a water mill, near the station, with boats on the mill stream, a bridge and fishing, wild flowers, trees, and the river Yar. A hamlet called *Kern*, to the north, is blissfully on the way to nowhere – except Ashley Downs, which are magnificent. Although only just behind the tripper-belt of coast, this is still (1967) real country, with only a few intrusive bungalows.

Appuldurcombe House [14]. A sad orange Palladian shell, preserved and exhibited by the Ministry of Works. It was for 300 years the seat of the Worsleys, perhaps the greatest of the old Island families. The name means the "valley of the apple-trees", and it is most beautifully placed in wooded country, facing east, with the high down behind it, and on this an obelisk put up in 1774 by Sir Richard Worsley to the memory of Sir Robert.

The site had been an alien priory, but passed to the Frys, the Leighs, and then by marriage to the Worsleys. The great house was built in 1710 by Sir Robert Worsley, who tidied away the Tudor manor-house which then existed to make the one really ambitious Palladian mansion of the Island: stately Corinthian pilasters in the height of fashion and, rather ostentatiously, a room for every week of the year and a window for every day.

The shell of
APPULDURCOMBE HOUSE,
near WROXALL

The Manor at ARRETON

There were four regular fronts of freestone, pilasters and ornaments of Portland stone, tiles of Westmorland slates, and inside, rich panelling, Adam fireplaces, and some of the window-frames in copper. Capability Brown laid out the grounds. Sir Richard Worsley lived here with a priceless collection of pictures and antiques from all over the world, and in 1784 published his History of the Wight, which remains a chief source of information about the Island. The direct line failed, and the estate fell to the first Earl of Yarborough, Baron Worsley of Appuldurcombe, the founder Commodore of the Royal Yacht Squadron. After his death the whole estate went, in 1846, under the hammer, and the treasures were scattered. The beautiful classical house became a school, a temporary monastery, and then the Germans dropped a landmine practically on it in 1943.

The shell is beautifully kept, and the once magnificent lawns are rough but tidy. All the interior decoration is gone: the walls are bare: the roofs gape open to the sky: only the stone contours are left, and the lodge, where you buy your ticket.

Arreton [7]. A charming straggling village in the East Medina, not badly spoilt by being on the main road from Newport to Sandown. At Downend, to the north, is the site of another Roman villa, and the Hare & Hounds inn, old, thatched, and with gibbet memories. Above is Arreton Down (444 ft.) with prodigious views both north and south.

The village is sheltered, with the classic grouping of church, manor-house, and farm, all together amongst trees. The manor-house is one of the noblest in the Island,

on a site originally belonging to Quarr Abbey. It was built in the early 17th century, and architecturally has never gone downhill. It is beautifully proportioned, of clean mellowed stone, with two gabled wings and a central porch: mullions, a terraced garden below, and Jacobean chimneys clustered above. Fine panelling inside, and altogether delightful. The farm has a pond with willows, and two large barns, a new Dutch one and one old and thatched.

The church, just below the Manor by a path, or up another from the inn on the main road, was fiercely restored in 1886, but has Saxon work in the east wall and examples of most subsequent periods. There are some dominating polished Purbeck columns. The huge buttresses outside the tower, making it look as fortified as Shalfleet, were put there as support when the steeple was struck down by lightning about 1500.

Atherfield [12]. Little Atherfield and Atherfieldgreen, on the south-west coast, consist of stone farms and cottages scattered over the low ground which stretches between the downs and the military road above Atherfield Point and Chale Bay. The shore is bleak and is mainly undeveloped, with much legend of wreckers and smugglers. By Atherfield Ledge twenty-four sailing ships once came to grief in twenty-four hours. The trees, as in the Scillies and parts of Cornwall, grow stunted and shrinking from the sea winds. There are good views back towards Freshwater. Some chalets operate in the summer.

Bembridge [9]. The easternmost village of the Island: really a developed and protected shoulder

of land jutting out below Brading Harbour, and gazing across towards Spithead. It is sheltered on the north and west by the marshes of St Helens, and by the Downs to the south. It is residential, and comparatively free from mass exploitation by day-trippers, but famous amongst yachtsmen everywhere. "Redwings" are always about in the bay or the harbour, and the Bembridge Sailing Club's important Clubhouse is prominent on the Toll Road from the north. The Royal Spithead is a large hotel, and modern, rather Thames-valley, houses are increasing in most directions away from the sea. Lane End, once a separate hamlet, is now a suburb. There are still a few old cottages about, and one or two marine villas. The new houses sometimes have large gardens with cedars, firs, and exotic borders. A windmill of 1900, at the end of the High Street, is much visited: the architecturally unimportant church, in Lake End Road, not so much: there are some antique shops. A self-contained yachting centre of active, but private interests, gratefully cut off from the coach-stream.

The reclaimed land to the southeast is almost the only level of any extent on the Island, and is the site of Bembridge Airport. The obelisk on Bembridge Down, to the first Earl of Yarborough, is of light stone which catches the sunlight and is visible for miles. So is the tower of Bembridge School, which has an important collection of Ruskin's works and pictures. South, round Whitecliff Bay, *Culver Cliff* stands up, very impressive from the sea. Like many young men, Swinburne scaled it – as a test of personal courage – in 1854. He succeeded at the second attempt, passed out in a coma, and in a dramatic letter explained how he was revived by a sheep poking its nose

Villas at BEMBRIDGE

BEMBRIDGE: The Sailing Club

RYDE ☞

into his face. It is perhaps named after the culver pigeons which used to flock here, and was remarkable in the 17th century for a rare breed of hawks.

Binstead [8]. Once a pretty village, famous for the quarries, now exhausted, which gave the stone for its own Quarr Abbey (q.v.) and for Winchester Cathedral and elsewhere. Now a suburb of Ryde, separated from it by strip-development and the Golf Links. The Church of the Holy Cross, near the shore, is amongst trees: rebuilt in 1844, but with early reminders. There is an "ancient symbolic stone" ("the Idol") over the porch doorway, and admired gravestones of a smuggler, an early parson, and Samuel Landon, the "biggest man in the world", when he died in 1844. A pretty strip of shore along Ryde Roads towards the monastery woods.

Blackgang Chine [17]. This, lying below St Catherine's Hill, half a mile from Chale, and on the most dangerous coast of the Island, was for centuries a place of fear to sailors, and a resort for gulls, and, at some point, the "black gang" of smugglers. To the early Victorian romantics it represented the pitch of terror and grandeur, and was a place of "savage sublimity", much engraved with a wreck in the foreground and the wrath of God striking black above the towering crags. It is now a Disneyland, of deep interest to the connoisseur of commercialization: a Niagara Falls in (as so much of the Island) miniature.
The gorge remains: a cleft in the rock caused by a stream, winding less far inshore than the chines at Shanklin or Luccombe, but much deeper. One side reaches 400 ft. The cliffs are of dark blue clay laced with yellow sandstone, and there is much beauty all about. From the Observation Peak 400 ft. up from the sea the view stretches beyond the Needles on one side to Bournemouth and the

RYDE: Victorian urban development

Isle of Wight Gothic at North Wells, BEMBRIDGE

Dorset coast: on the other to St Catherine's Point.
The chine is owned by the Dabell family. It was acquired and developed by Alexander Dabell in 1843, the height of the Island's boom period, and is still managed, with increasing enterprise but a fine sense of continuity, by his descendants. Behind the car park, the rustic fencing, the turnstiles and the restaurant are paths and gardens in terraces, and infinite attractions: a Hall of Mirrors, a Smugglers' Cave, a floodlit water garden and a model of Shanklin Old Village which looks rather more genuine than the original. There is a quintessential Gnomes' Garden and a maze, whose hedges it is estimated, far-

sightedly, will be fully grown by 1970. A museum contains infinite wonders, including a collection of ships in bottles and the entire skeleton of a Greenland whale, wrecked on the Island in 1845. Also much about other wrecks from the Bay below, where over 180 vessels have been lost since 1750. The greatest wonder is the bazaar, which contains every sort of souvenir, and the Island specialities of sands and shells used with brain-racked ingenuity. Blackgang is, to taste, exhilarating or, although not in the sense in which an 1832 guidebook used the words, "grand and gloomy".

Blackwater [7] on the Medina River was a hundred years ago

lyrically desribed as "a region of the thickest shade, where antique and decayed oaks expose their half-naked roots from both the banks". Now a nexus of crossings on the main Newport – Godshill road, with pretty trees and ugly houses. St George's Down (363 ft.), with fine views of the Medina and Yar Valleys, lies above it to the east, and there are good walks to Gatcombe and Arreton.

Bonchurch [18]. Victorian panegyrists and trippers' puffs tumble with ecstatic adjectives about the natural beauties. In spite of all commercialism, these still exist, and even the beach is not spoilt. There are modern houses, tea shops and curios, but it is still a small place, blessed by nature and civilized by Victorians. It is an eastern suburb of Ventnor, but an unexpected one, timbered, watered and luxurious. It was a parish when Ventnor was a few cottages. The village lies in the lap of the Undercliff. Bonchurch Pond is a pool by the side of the road, framed by trees. It was presented by H. de Vere Stacpoole, of "The Blue Lagoon", who lived here. Amongst the rocks above and opposite to it are small villas in their own grounds, perched at all levels and reached by narrow climbing lanes, with steep bends in them. The Undercliff climbs up to Upper Bonchurch 400 ft above, lush with vegetation, and with runnels of water cascading down. The old church is a tiny building, originally Norman, with hallowed but unexciting additions. It is dedicated to St Boniface, and traditionally the scene of his missionary work. The priests of the Abbey of Lyra are supposed to have landed at Monks Bay, below, to bring Christianity to the Island in AD 755. In the flowery churchyard is buried the Rev. William Adams, author of the improving best-seller "The Shadow of the Cross".
De Vere Stacpoole is buried at the new church, built typically in 1847,

BLACKGANG CHINE

Marine Villa at BONCHURCH

and the roll-call of notables who stayed in Bonchurch includes Tennyson, Dickens, Thackeray, Macaulay, the "Punch" artists John Leech and Dicky Doyle, Anna Sewell, who wrote "Black Beauty" and Sir John Martin-Harvey. It retains an aura of Great Victorians in undress: an overcrowded corner of social history.

ST BONIFACE DOWN, above Bonchurch, is 221 acres of dominating downland stretching from behind Ventnor to join Shanklin Down,

and visible from all over the Island. Its summit is 787 ft., the highest point in the Island. It has tumuli, for those who wish a Wishing Well, and there are glorious views in all directions. It belongs to the National Trust.

Brading [9]. Not synthetic, but over-cried as a stop for visitors, who are pointed out the old Town Hall (restored) by the church, with its stocks and whipping-post, and a bull-ring by a lamp-post nearer the station. The village itself is a straggling main street

of unobtrusive houses, running tightly uphill to the church. It has spread to take in visitors and new residents, with modern villas and terraces, guest houses and bungalows, and is now a large modernized village, full of motor-traffic. Thatched and stone houses and occasional Regency villas are tucked away above it.

Historically Brading (the "broad meadow") had some importance: it was the "King's Town", with a harbour, very early charters renewed by Edward VI, and the return of two members of Parliament. The flat marshy land to the east, now some 650 acres of low farm land, full of water-birds, was sea. Small vessels came up to the quay at Brading, with the tide, until 1880. The fight for reclamation had gone on through history, to be finally won with the making of an embankment across the harbour in 1878, which left Brading cut off from the sea. The church (St Mary), although drastically restored, is the oldest in the Island, allegedly founded by St Wilfrid, who sailed up Brading Harbour to convert the Jutes. It is Norman-Transitional, with an Early English tower and chancel. The foot of the tower is unusually pierced with arches to facilitate processions round the church without leaving consecrated ground. The most attractive thing inside is in the Oglander Chapel, with the tombs of the Oglanders of Nunwell. It contains a coloured wooden effigy of Sir William Oglander, 1608, recumbent and gaily staring upward. This, and a replica of it for his son, set in a wall niche above, are figures which Sir William had admired in life, and kept in Nunwell library for the express purpose of being put here at his death. In severe contrast is a brass memorial to the Rev. Leigh Richmond, non-resident vicar from 1797 to 1805, who wrote the "Annals of the Poor", and the grave of Jane the Young Cottager, who appears in it.

Morton Road, just off the Sandown Road, leads to the remains of the *Roman Villa*. This is much the most interesting Roman evidence in the Island, and has well-preserved mosaics, a hypocaust, and various other antiquities, displayed and explained. It must have been a villa of some importance, and was occupied late – well into the 5th century. Its description as "a miniature Pompeii" is, however, Wight magniloquence.

NUNWELL MANOR is half a mile west, at the foot of Brading Down, half-hidden from the road. It has been the home of the Oglander family ever since the first Richard d'Orglandes attended

CALBOURNE: The much visited Winkle Street

William Fitz-Osborne at the Conquest. The direct line died out in 1874, but the connection and name persist. Their fame is perhaps the best known of all Wight families because of the private memoirs of the royalist Sir John Oglander, who died in 1655. The published extracts ("Nunwell Symphony") are fascinating. So are the house and grounds: less imposing than the great Appuldurcombe of the Worsleys must have been, but, like any continuously inhabited house, a palimpsest of styles, with a Georgian brick façade over the earlier stone. If not the best of the Island houses, this is one of the most famous, and still in private hands. Henry VIII stayed here with the Oglanders, Charles I dined when a prisoner at Carisbrooke, and so have generations of Island gentry.

Brighstone [12]. A resort village on the visitors' circuit, with car park,

souvenirs, tea-gardens, and a row of decorative cottages almost as photographed as "Winkle Street". In spite of this, and several hideous buildings in the main street, it remains a cheerful village, with some pleasant typical Wight stone and thatched cottages. It is beautifully placed on a sunny tableland with wooded hills above it to the north, and a stream and chine down to the Undercliff, across the Military Road to the south.

The church, among trees, has a good square tower with a little dunce's cap steeple. Inside, Victorian Decorated instead of the original Perpendicular but a good Jacobean pulpit and agreeable churchyard. Three famous rectors: Bishop Ken, who wrote the hymns, from 1667 to 1669, and Samuel Wilberforce and George Moberly, who became Victorian bishops. Brick development along the main roads: a holiday camp

nearby, and fine views from the downs.

It is pronounced, and was often written, Brixton, and was the town of Ecbright, who gave it to the see of Winchester in 826.

Brook [11] has a bleak face to the Undercliff and Brook Bay, some three miles from Freshwater along the windswept Military Road. At Hanover Point, just before you reach the turning up into Brook, is the Pine Raft – the fossilized remains of a primeval pine forest, spooky or scientific, to taste, with petrified trunks visible at low water.

Climbing inland into the village the trees are less dwarfed by the wind, and the slope becomes forested as it mounts towards the downs. The village is in a hollow,

St Catherine's Lighthouse,
NITON

with seemly Island cottages on both sides of the road. Standing back is Brook House. It is a Palladian building on the site of an earlier manor where Henry VII was entertained by a Dame Joanna Bowerman. In this one Garibaldi, who planted an authentic Wellingtonia here, was entertained by the Seelys. It was the first Lord Mottistone's father who built the new Brook Hill house, high up above the village. He did so in 1914, having a prevision of life at ground level with the development of the internal combustion engine. This house, which was for a few years the home of Mr J. B. Priestley, stands amongst exotic foliage and a sheet of rhododendrons, magnificently viewing, and to be viewed from, several miles of the road ringing the south-west of the Island.

The Church (St Mary the Virgin) stands away from the village on a little hill, beside the road north to Shalcombe, and is full of monuments to the Bowermans, formerly lords of the manor, and to death by drowning.

Calbourne [6]. A debouchment for visitors to Winkle Street, but a pretty if not outstanding village of stone and thatched cottages on a hill up from the bourne at the bottom, with the Westover Estate lying the other side of it, behind trees. The church is well-placed, with a green in front, and is basically 13th century, with a pleasant rectory behind it, basically Tudor. Both are heavily restored. The church has some good brasses.

"Winkle Street" itself is a row of tiled and thatched cottages lying beside a stream with a pretty bridge at the bottom of the village. It is over-photographed and inevitably self-conscious, but in spite of some bottle-glass not aggressively olde. Nice cottages, flowerbeds, and a stream, unkindly inflated into a show piece village. SWAINSTONE (pronounced Swanston) is another large estate lying

NITON: the lighthouse keepers' houses at St Catherine's Point

back from the road towards Newport. The name recalls the Danish theme in the history of Wight, and Sweyn, father of Canute. The house was damaged by bombs in 1941, but much remains, with a 13th century hall in the large grounds, behind the cedars of Lebanon. Tennyson came here to visit his friend Sir John Simeon, and to write "Maud".

Carisbrooke [7] is commercially restrained. In spite of a now continuous stretch of houses it is not absorbed as a suburb of Newport, technically a mile away to the east, nor is it simply an amenity centre for the castle which rises above it, with its constant stream of visitors. For centuries it was the capital of the Island. But it remains a village in spite of out-

lying development and light industry, with a long street, all of unexceptional but agreeable stone and brick houses running uphill to Alvington Shute past the church from the brook and footbridge at the bottom. It was originally Buccombe, or Beaucombe, the fair valley, and it is still possible to see why.

The church (St Mary) is the best in the Island. It was originally attached to a nearby Cistercian priory, and was one of the original ten churches in the Island mentioned in Domesday. The monks, of the Lyra Fraternity, were unpopular after the French raids, and were removed. Henry V suppressed the priory altogether, and there is nothing of it left to see. No doubt there was a Saxon building here, and the Norman one may well have been started by

A rustic conceit near COWES

the Fitz-Osborne who also began work on the castle. The present building, stone and brick outside, in a good churchyard, is a palimpsest: Norman, 14th century east windows, an arcade of transition arches, repairs by Sir Francis Walsingham when he was Lay Rector, miscellaneous windows, all restored in 1907, and with church furniture from Princess Beatrice. The pulpit is Cromwellian, and there are interesting effigies. On the north outside of the church are some graffiti of the 15th century, discovered in 1907 and to be found behind glass and grass, on the plaster of the wall. They are rather charming, but do not look as if they will last another five hundred years. Above it all is the fine 14th century tower, with five stages.

A steep path goes up from the village to the backcloth, the castle.

CARISBROOKE CASTLE [7]. A place of organized pilgrimage, covering a plateau of about twenty acres; partly castle and partly car park, reached a hundred and fifty feet up above the village, grouped classically beneath it. It stands well, and there are fine views from the walls. It is entirely altered from the ivy-hung romantic ruin of Keats' admiration, although there are still jackdaws, and it perhaps never was as menacingly picturesque as in the Victorian steel-engravings. It is clinically garnished by the Ministry of Works, who also sell admirable literature for those interested in fortress architecture or Carolean martyrology.

There may have been a neolithic settlement at Carisbrooke, and there was certainly a small Roman fort. Traces are pointed out on the bank near the castle entrance. William Fitz-Osborne, the first commander of the Island, began the Norman work, and there were additions throughout the Middle Ages, but what you see is mainly the great reconstruction work of the Italian engineer Genebella, who also built Tilbury fort. His curtain walls enclose the full 20 acres, as opposed to the acre and a half of the original fortress. The

work was done in 245 days as a crash job to meet the Armada threat, mainly by local volunteer labour. Carisbrooke is really a Tudor ruin, with some medieval interior work still preserved. Its popular legend is of Charles I's imprisonment here in 1647, his attempts to escape, and the subsequent death in the castle of his daughter Elizabeth (see Historical Note, pp. 15-16).

Through an outer gateway (E.R. 1598) at the top of well-photographed steps are inner wooden gates of 1470, and inside is the base-court, with firm directions and maps of what is to be seen. There are *garrison quarters* on the left, and steps up to the *Ramparts* and the views. The *Keep*, on an artificial mound 58 ft. high, is reached by seventy-one steps and a handrail. It is the oldest bit of the castle, and an unusually preserved example of this sort of Norman building. It looks down outside onto the *Bowling Green*, converted to this use for Charles I in 1648, but previously the tilt-yard of the castle. It was used until recently for garrison review purposes, and has seen much history.

From the Keep, looking down inside the walls, are lawns, administrative buildings, and the main block, drastically but tactfully repaired by Hardwicke in 1905, which includes the *Governor's House*. This was until 1940 occupied by the Governor when in residence. It is now the museum for the Island, small but well-arranged, and especially the home of Stuart relics: lace, signet-ring, lock of hair. The part of the building nearest the North Wall used to be the Great Hall, and Charles I was here until his first attempt to escape. The *Well House* is the show incident of the castle, and enormously popular relief for most children. Others cry. It is a restored 16th century building over a well sunk in 1150, after the castle had once fallen to the French for lack of water. The hole is 161 ft. deep, and the average depth of water is 40 ft. There are donkeys who do a turn drawing up the water by bucket,

using a tread-mill. They have an easy life, and achieve well-advertised longevity.

Near the gatehouse is the modern *Chapel of St Nicholas in Castro*, consecrated in 1905, now the *Isle of Wight Memorial*. There was a Norman chapel here. Ruined, it was rebuilt in 1738, and again dismantled in 1856. The present building is a reproduction of the sanctuary at the time of Charles I's imprisonment, built on the original base by Percy G. Stone. Queen Victoria gave a bronze bust of Charles I, and there are other royal endowments, much light and coloured decoration.

Like the Parthenon, the castle is worth the climb, in spite of the publicity.

Chale [17]. A scattered village at the "Back of the Wight", on the great military road. It has a few nondescript houses and a church (St Andrew) with the downs standing grandly behind it. The church is a bleak building with a Perpendicular Tower (1538, renovated 1958) and a graveyard with tombs that are said to have been used as storage vaults by smugglers, and two mounting stones for a portly Victorian clergyman. To the east, under St Catherine's Hill, is the old Manor House, now called Chale Abbey Farm, with 14th century and Tudor work and nearby a fine 15th century barn.

All the coast here is warm and bracing in summer, and there are camps and "facilities". But it is also notoriously dangerous for shipping, and Chale Bay used to be called the Bay of Death. It was a haunt of wreckers. The trees, like Cornish ones, shrink inland, away from the wind, and it is desolate in wintertime.

Up the road north it is softer country again and *Chale Green* is a few cottages in an open and agreeable setting, quite different in character.

Chillerton [13]. A long straggling village in the heart of the interior, and, for the Island, mercifully peaceful and unfrequented. It is

CARISBROOKE: the Castle

mixed cottages, running along a stream, and in a hollow between the downs, in places 500 ft high, with barrows, earthworks, and lychets. Just to the north is *Sheat*, a gabled Tudor farmhouse behind a good wrought-iron gateway. South is *Billingham Manor*, part Jacobean and part Georgian.

Colwell Bay [4]. A stretch of resort round a fine curving bay about two miles long, that was once known only to families who made annual pilgrimage to their own pitches, and is now a recreation-strip. It lies partly in the parish of Totland, and partly in Freshwater, off the main road from Yarmouth and round the western point of the Island. A pub, guest house, villas, a miniature golf course, safe bathing with proprietary beach huts, and a car park with a slipway to the beach. Motor-boat trips to the Needles and just the place for a holiday camp. There is one. There are shells, too, and fossils much described, but now no oyster beds.

Cowes [2]. Internationally famous as the headquarters of yacht-racing, and, from the sea, always busy. Cowes is the chief entrance to the Island from Southampton, $11\frac{1}{2}$ miles northwest, and is really two ports connected by a floating bridge over the Medina River. West Cowes is white, and yachts; East Cowes is grey, and industry. There are fanciful origins for the name, but probably it is from a sandbank called "the Cow", the East and West attaching after the respective forts built by Henry VIII. There have been shipyards here since the 12th century, and great ships for the Royal Navy were built and fitted here in the 18th century (incidentally adding cause for the deforestation of the Island.)

🐟 *COWES: the High Street*

COWES:
(above) *Holy Trinity Church,
the Solent House School*
(below) *From the jetty of
the Royal Yacht Squadron*

The frontage from the sea shows the famous but tiny Parade, with a stone balustrade. The most obvious feature is a shiny block of cement flats, but the general effect is animated and agreeable. The Royal Yacht Squadron, the capital of the yachting world, is technically on Victoria Parade. It became the headquarters in 1856, and the terrace retains the circular gun platform which is all that is left of the 16th century castle. Nearby is Holy Trinity Church, which was built in 1832, the period of various marine buildings down the front to crenellated Egypt Point, on the west and leading to Gurnard. Here is Princes Green, secured from commercial exploitation by a gift of 1863, which has some attractive marine villas above it. It leads into Princes Esplanade. Egypt Point itself has a flashing light, visible for ten miles. A boom from here stretched across the Solent during the war, to Stone Point on the mainland. Behind the front are narrow winding streets, mostly one way, with some balcony houses and bow-fronted shops "by Royal Appointment": seaside with Regency and Victorian undertones. As the town grows up and away from the sea it becomes more modern, and fringes inland with bungalows. The Roman Catholic Church of 1796 in Terminus Road has some Italian paintings, and Northwood House (Nash-like, but not by him) is now the civic centre. It has magnificent grounds, filled with tourist amenities and rare trees. There is a plaque for Dr Arnold's birthplace in Birmingham Road (he did indeed love the Island) and another, on the parade, for the first British settlers for Maryland, who left in 1633. Yacht racing (the word is Dutch, and means a hunting-dog) goes on from the beginning of May till the end of September, peaking for Cowes Week at the beginning of August, when eight clubs take part. There is a record of a regatta in 1776, and the Yacht Club was formed in 1815. The Prince Regent patronized the sport, and the Club was renamed the Royal Yacht Club

when he became King, altering again to the Royal Yacht Squadron in honour of his brother, William IV, in 1833. But the golden and exclusive days were those up to 1914. Now yachting is rather more democratic, and club-houses pepper the shore in wood and brick profusion, and the roads with sails.

EAST COWES. In spite of its attractive approach, an ugly sea-port, with back streets that might be Belfast or Rotherhithe. The best views are from the water-frontages: of wharves, cranes and warehouses on piles, with Norris Castle and the hill above old Castle Point away to the east. Historically the chief industry is ship-building, including the construction of life-boats, but there is also an aircraft industry, with a cocooned Princess Flying Boat on the opposite bank to the ferry, a hovercraft factory, a gas station and electrical generating plant.

The esplanade winds round rather disconsolately to the foot of the grounds of Norris Castle to the east, under woods and lawns, and on to Osborne. Above, East Cowes is more attractive. Nothing is left of the Tudor fort, but Norris Castle stands finely from the sea. It was built by James Wyatt for Lord Seymour in 1790, and is still in private hands. It is mock-medieval, and largely for show, but has dignity and fine grounds stretching down to the sea. Until recently it was adjoined by East Cowes Castle, which John Nash built for himself in 1798. This was an extravagance of the picturesque, and engravings of it are for sale or admiration all over the Island. Unfortunately it has now been demolished, and on the estate are new bungalows and "units" in "John Nash Avenue" and "York Avenue". Nash himself was a successful developer, and would no doubt understand. He is buried in the church (St James) which he himself designed, very plainly, half a mile away.

Fishbourne [3]. Well-known because the car-ferry arrives here from Portsmouth. The creek is

wooded and pretty, the houses mainly modern, some round a cheerful pocket green: Thames Valley by the sea. It is a fishing hamlet that was first a painter's piece, then "discovered" and is now developing fast toward nautical suburbanity.

Farringford [10], a large basically eighteenth century house, is set back from Bedbury Lane, just outside Freshwater, woodfringed and off the main road to Alum Bay. It is a hotel, and the Tennyson connection is observed but not obtruded. The poet lived happily here for thirty years, after buying the property in 1852, and much of his work, including "Maud", "The Idylls of the King", and "Enoch Arden", was completed in an attic he called his "fumitory". What is now the dining-room was his children's playroom and the drawing-room has wonderful views of the bay, framed by the trees of the grounds, which are lovely and well-kept. Jenny Lind sang here, Sullivan played, and a procession of eminent Victorians visited Tennyson, whilst a Wellingtonia on the lawn was allegedly (but dubiously) planted by Garibaldi. Most of the minor Tennysonia are now in the museum at Carisbrooke. But there is "Tennyson's bridge", and the pathway to the Downs and the Tennyson monument, which is granite and can be seen from all over the Island. The High Down belongs to the National Trust, and the views are magnificent. Tennyson needed that cape: it is always windy.

Freshwater [5]. The old village consists of a few houses round the church, which stands on a hill overlooking the Yar at the end of the estuary. It is about a mile inland, and everything to the west of it is called the Freshwater peninsula. The church (All Saints) has a 15th century tower, looking down the street, but the inside was inflated by new aisles

The ferry between East and West COWES

38

The cliffs at FRESHWATER BAY: Tennyson Down in the background

and generally reconstituted in 1873. Tennyson was buried in Westminster Abbey, but Lady Tennyson is in the churchyard and there are memorials to the family.

Most of Freshwater is resort suburban, with almost every building a guest-house. But there are shaded lanes linking the formerly separate hamlets of *School Green, Sheepwash Green,* (one origin of the still extant surname Sheepwash) and *Pound Green,* with a remaining village pound amongst some pretty cottages.

FRESHWATER BAY. is part of the parish of Freshwater, and lies to its south, looking out on to the English Channel. The tiny bay, geologically recent, has a pebbly beach beneath a brief ledge of esplanade with a hotel. On its east are an Arch Rock, a Stag rock with an improbable legend, and some good caves. In 1799 there existed here nothing but an inn called the "Cabin", where George Morland stayed, sketched, and hobnobbed with smugglers and fishermen. Now there are villas of most subsequent periods, marine terraces and hotels, with a golf links to the east on Afton Down, and the beginning of the Military Road.

There is a pretty thatched church at Freshwater Gate, with a misleading stone inserted, with 1693 on it, and some nice woodwork in the chancel. It was built in 1908, on land given by the Tennysons.

Gatcombe [13]. A pretty secluded spot, and the name probably means the "gateway to the valley", where it stands. It is only four miles from Newport, but a true village, unintruded, with stone and thatch cottages, leafy trees and a stream. It lies below the church and the great house, which are away up a drive through a valley, amongst trees, and facing a farmstead on the other side.

The church is mainly 13th century, with a 15th century tower, last restored by Sir Charles Seely in 1922, and beautifully kept. There is a somewhat inexplicable wooden effigy of a knight in armour (Jacobean?) in the chancel, and a life-size marble monument by Brock to Charles Grant Seely, who was killed on active service at Gaza in 1917, in the nave. Already it has been defaced by an iconoclast. There is a Mental Hospital to the north, which has a somewhat defacing clock-tower, seen from the road to Newport.

The House, which belongs to the National Trust, was another seat of the great Worsley family. It stands in a luxurious park with plane trees, and was intended as an unostentatious pocket edition of Appuldurcombe, when its Palladian façade was built in 1756. Parts of the back are older. Latterly it belonged to the Seely family.

Godshill [13]. A very pretty village disfigured by its anxiety to please. Once a quiet inland place, its position on the main road from Newport to the coast, and its genuine charm, have made it an exclamation mark for sightseers. The trim thatched cottages are punctuated by tea shops, and some draw attention by signs to their unremarkable dates. Quaint shops

sell curios and pottery. There is a gnome village by the Old Smithy, and a model village in the garden of the Old Rectory. It is all highly self-conscious.

A row of much-photographed cottages by the church are indeed attractive, and the village is beautifully placed amongst leafy lanes. The gardens have sub-tropical plants. The church (excellently documented) stands at the top of a steep little incline, supposedly placed there by miraculous agency (Godshill by this interpretation meaning "Idol Hill"). It is essentially Perpendicular work with nice carved springers and bosses in the south transept, and a 15th century wall painting of "Christ crucified on a budding tree", on the east wall. Also a "Daniel in the Lions' Den", optimistically attributed to Rubens, in the nave. A fine 16th century monument to Sir John Leigh and his wife, and numerous memorials to his Worsley suc-

cessors at Appuldurcombe House, nearby.

Gurnard [2]. A resort extension of Cowes, to the west: a bungalow town, huts, hotels, guest houses, a front with a putting-green, an Esplanade. Roman and Victorian remains, but essentially a cheerful contemporary seaside development for bathing and boating. The front goes round, bleak and windswept in winter, to Egypt Point. The country immediately inland from it is ordinary, but well wooded to the west. A large holiday camp.

Kingston [13]. A few cottages and an undistinguished church hidden on a little hill just off the corner at Beckfield Cross, between Chale Green and Shorwell, and the smallest parish in the Island. The church (St James) is a very small Early English one, with only a bell-cote on top of it, all completely re-done in 1871. Enjoyable

FRESHWATER BAY: The Arch Rock

COWES: The chain ferry across the Medina

from its setting, which is high above another splendid manor-house and great home farm, hidden at the foot of the hill the other side from the road. Inside is a good brass memorial to a Richard Mewys of 1535, and the Meux, or Mews (the name means beer to many inn signs) lived in the manor for centuries. This is Jacobean; stone, with a fine chimney of 18th-century brick-work. It is hidden and unextolled, but one of the finest domestic buildings in the Island, in wooded undesecrated country.

Lake [14]. A length of the enter-tainment strip on the sheltered east coast, merging into Sandown on the north and Shanklin to the south. It has a fine late Victorian church (The Good Shepherd) designed by Temple Moore and built in 1892. There is a cliff-top walk with good views, and a sea-front. Along the back lies the railway, the main coast road, and development.

Luccombe [14]. The village is for the motorist a dead end on the coast, a mile south of Shanklin. This and a steep descent preserve the *Chine*, formed by a small stream, from mass intrusion, and the ravine remains wilder and to some therefore more attractive than Shanklin chine to the north. Overlooking Luccombe Common and the landslip is Nansen Hill, fifteen acres of heather and gorse-land given to the National Trust in 1934. All splendid walking country.

THE LANDSLIP stretches along the coast from Luccombe Chine to Dunnose Point, and is a famous beauty spot of tangled trees and undergrowth. It maintains a remoteness, however, and is luxuriant and comparatively un-tamed. There are rough stone steps down from the road to the Upper Landslip, twisted oaks and dense hazel thickets, with paths and a watch-tower. The Lower

Landslip has a Smugglers' Path, caves, rocks, and a wilderness of coast leading on to Monks Bay and Bonchurch. Everywhere there are rocks and the natural debris of the great landslip of 1818, constantly assisted by lesser later ones. The cliff towers above, and the sun comes through in splashes. It is luxuriant, full of charm and wild flowers.

Merstone [13]. A sparse hamlet a mile south-west of Arreton, on a by-road: a farm or so, a tiny Methodist Chapel, and cottages. Unexpectedly down a lane is Merstone Manor and a large farm, charmingly hidden by trees. The manor is a beautiful Jacobean house, unusually built of deep red brick, with stone windows and doorways. The local antiquarian, Percy Stone, whose writings preserve much of the Island, and who died in 1934, lived at Merstone Cottage.

Mottistone [12]. The Manor House and the church face each other across the main inland road from West Wight to the east, with a steep wooded cliff behind, up to the downs.

The Manor House has 1559 over the doorway (with a Latin inscription by the first Lord Birkenhead) and the building is in fact mainly 16th century. Much of it was buried alive about two hundred years ago by a landslip of the fault above, when some fifteen hundred tons of earth came down leaving little but the chimneys showing. There were farm buildings, but when the first Lord Mottistone and his architect son excavated and restored it in 1926 it romantically emerged as a mellow and beautiful L-shaped Tudor building in virtually pure condition. It is now used as three homes, including the Rectory, but remains a striking and conspicuous piece of 16th century domestic architecture.

The church was extensively and expensively restored in the 19th century, but is beautifully kept. It preserves much 12th and 14th century work and has an early font, a Jacobean pulpit, and an 18th century organ by John

LUCCOMBE: The beach and village above

England. There are Mottistone memorials in the Cheke Chapel. The Manor originally belonged to the Chekes, best-known for the Sir John Cheke who was tutor to Edward VI.

A gateway opposite the church leads to a path going steeply up behind the manor, through the woods, to the Long Stone. This is a pillar of iron sandstone 13 ft high with another lying at its foot, the Island's only megalith. It is regarded as surviving from a long barrow of about 2,500 BC. The cliff goes on above it to reach over 600 ft. There is to the east a fortified camp called Castle Hill, with magnificent views to the south-east and St Catherine's Down.

Newbridge [6]. A straggling twisty village with some pleasant stone and brick cottages in undisfigured countryside. It remains agreeable in spite of a caravan site and being on the lower road from Yarmouth to Newport.

Newchurch [14]. This was once a large parish spreading right across the Island, and including the then hamlets of Ryde and Ventnor. It has stood still as the Island developed into a resort, and now the church is served from Arreton. It is a cheerful village of thatched cottages with flower gardens, the main street undefiled, perched on a hill in delightful country. North is Mersley Down (413 ft.) and east is wooded farmland stretching to Sandown and the coast. Borthwood Copse, 58 acres of woodland to the south-east, belongs to the National Trust.

All Saints is plain (the "new" in Newchurch means Norman) but well-set at the top of the village. The inside, restored but not overtittivated for tourists, has the usual early wooden pulpit of the old Island churches, with sounding board dated 1700, a lectern, "the pelican in its piety", which was once at Frome in Somerset,

and interesting lancet windows in the north wall of the chancel. The wooden tower is unusual, modern and handsome.

Newport [7]. The capital of the Island, near the middle of it, and the only town not on the coast. Even so the river Medina, bisecting the Island from here to the north, allows quite large ships up to the busy but unexciting harbour. As a result the streets are usually crowded with traffic, circulating round the bus station and car park which constitute the operational centre. The streets are those of any busy little country town, and it takes Sunday or heavy rain to reveal that the overall height of the buildings and the general proportions are much as they were in the steel engravings of the early Victorian period.

Then there was a gay social life of Island families, with routs, assemblies, reviews and most of the amenities of a provincial town on the mainland.

Earlier there may have been a Roman settlement, and a ruined villa remains in suburban Avondale Road. The town was given a charter and became the "new port" in 1180, but derived its authority from Carisbrooke. It emerged into history only when suffering from plague, the Black Death, or incursions by the French, who sacked it in 1377. It was described as "a poor sort of place" by Sir John Oglander in the 16th century, and the records for the time of Charles I's negotiations there with the Parliamentarians are notably absent. It sent two members to Parliament from 1584 to 1885, but the more

*Part of the Manor House,
MOTTISTONE*

*NEWPORT:
Warehouses near the harbour*

eminent, like the Duke of Wellington and Palmerston, had nothing actually to do with the place.

Underneath the commercial preoccupation Newport retains a sense of independence, and seems self-reliant: the visitors go through it. The streets are regular, some (Quay Street and Sea Street) with nautical names, and with a few old houses, many Victorian ones, and some large art nouveau shops in the middle. The modern county offices in Lower High Street are good.

The old market square is now St James Square, with a verdigruesome memorial to Queen Victoria, and one or two pleasant buildings including the best in the town, Nash's Isle of Wight Institution, now the County Club, on the corner. Nash also designed the Guildhall, put up 1814–1816, which is spoilt by the addition of a clock-tower to commemorate the Jubilee. It stands well, however, in the High Street, and the interior, used for Quarter and other sessions, is excellent. It stands on the site of the old Town Hall where Charles I held negotiations with the Parliamentary Commissioners which resulted in the abortive Treaty of Newport of 1648. He lodged in the old Grammar School, built in 1619, and still extant, with high gables and mullioned windows, on the corner of St James Street and Lugley Street.

NEWPORT docks

NEWPORT: The Isle of Wight Institution designed, like the Town Hall, by John Nash

SHANKLIN

There are some attractive old inns. They include the Castle (1684), and the Bugle, now restored, but which was the headquarters of the Parliamentarians. "Bugle" (there is another in Yarmouth) is an old English word for "bull", and the origin of this curious surname. "God's Providence House", near the church, is a tea shop. It was so called because no one died there during the disastrous plague of 1584.

The church itself stands well in a little piazza, with a high pinnacled tower. In spite of the weathering the foundation stone was laid by the Prince Consort in 1854. It retains fittings from the older church on the site, which was decaying, and particularly a fine Jacobean pulpit of 1637, with two rows of heavily carved panels and a sounding-board. The font (1633) was discarded at the Restoration but later rescued from the vicarage garden. At the east end of the

 *The Town Hall at NEWTOWN*

north aisle is a pretty monument in Carrara marble to Princess Elizabeth, the 15 year old daughter of Charles I who died in Carisbrooke Castle. (A small model of it in the Museum is easier to appreciate.) It is by the Italian, Count Marichetti. Queen Victoria presented it, and also a bleak plaque of the Consort, which regards it. There is a fine Elizabethan monument to a Captain of the Island, Sir Edward Horsey.

There is the usual ugly if enterprising development round the edges of Newport, but a fine row of typical Victorian terraces on the road leading to Carisbrooke. Some houses in the town, and many in the Island, have rather nasty contrasting brick effects which seem indigenous.

The Seely County Library in Upper St James Street has a collection of Island literature.

Newtown [6]. This lies half a mile north of Shalfleet and the main road, on a marshy flat running out into the estuary creeks like salty fingers stretching in from Newtown Bay. The river was once far deeper, and would take fifty ships of five hundred tons. Then there was a salt industry and oyster beds, the latter recently revived. Newtown is indeed the most ancient borough of the Island, originally Francheville, a "free town" from manorial obligations. It was raided and burned by the French in 1377, and although rebuilt as the "new town" never fully recovered. However, it remained proud, and, a prize rotten borough, returned two members to Parliament until the Reform Act of 1832. There had been a famous fair, and there is a dialect song about the "Newtown Randy". But the harbour silted up, the town became only a few cottages, the roads, called Broad Street or High Street, subsided into leafy lanes, some of them farm paths covered in grass. A modest church (Holy Spirit), good of its sort, was put up in 1837. But of the former glories only the little Town Hall remained.

This was derelict, too, but was romantically rescued by philanthropic admirers, calling themselves "The Ferguson Gang", who anonymously subscribed for the repair and upkeep of the building in 1934, and gave it to the National Trust. It stands dramatically isolated on a patch of grass by the side of the road. It dates from 1699, and is a simple oblong structure with a stone base continued up in brick: a white portico and two windows in the front, and steps up the back. It is a delightful little building, and so are the cottages behind, with the old inn, and one or two unaggressive modern houses beside the lay-out of ghost-roads heavy with trees. The High Street peters out into a field path towards the deserted quay, the dead saltings, and the reeds amongst the alluvial mud. Across the estuary lie the gorse and woods of Lower Hamstead. It is pretty, romantic and (1967) unspoilt.

Niton [17]. Basically an undistinguished but pleasant village of miscellaneous houses lying back from St Catherine's Point. Now very much a staging post on the new southern road round to the resorts of East Medina. It was known until recently as Crab Niton. The church (St John the Baptist) is one of the original ten mentioned in Domesday Book. It has a squat Island spire on a 16th century tower, but is dull inside. *Undercliff Niton* is the newer extension down to the coast, with the charming Royal Sandrock Hotel where Queen Victoria stayed as a girl, and a pub called The Buddle. Also other hotels, and caravans. With the lighthouse below, and beautiful stretches of downs above, Niton is much visited and a popular centre, still with some rural character.

Northwood [2]. A spread of mainly modern buildings, though with good country round about it, on the main road from the prison end of Newport to Cowes and on the west side of the Medina. The church is dull, except for a good south doorway. It was once a

Chapelry of Carisbrooke and then the mother church of Cowes.

Norton [5] used to be a hamlet of a few scattered fishermen's houses to the south-west of Yarmouth, over the river embankment, and is now a strip of marine development on the way to Totland and the Needles. On the coast is the 19th century Fort Victoria. It is on the site of an earlier one from which Charles I was taken in 1648 en route for imprisonment at Hurst Castle, which juts out on the mainland opposite. A dim little garrison church, isolated on the main road, now serves virtually no one.

Osborne House [2]. Queen Victoria had this domestic palace built between 1845 and 1848 as a country retreat of some 2,000 acres to escape from crowds and ceremonial. It is on rising ground to the east of the Medina estuary. It was the Prince Consort's conception to build a modern Italian villa over the Solent, which he saw as the Bay of Naples. Thomas Cubitt was made responsible to him for the designs, and he used the latest construction methods, with cast-iron beams. Osborne is therefore not a grandiloquent climax of this sort of ornate Victorian architecture, but an exciting beginning: Cubitt employed its ideas extensively afterwards for the "Osborne style" of many London suburbs. There are two tall campaniles and a first floor loggia, and outside mock Renaissance terraces with a fountain and statues, leading down to the sea. Prince Albert filled the grounds with oaks, cedars, ash, and other English trees except for conifers near the house itself. Here, and elsewhere in the Island, there are still red squirrels.

Queen Victoria entertained at Osborne most of the visiting royalty of the world, and the Establishment of her reign. She died here on January 22nd 1901, and King Edward, for whom it had unhappy memories, promptly gave it to the nation. It is now administered by the Ministry of Public Works, and visited as

assiduously and with as proud wonder as the royal palaces in Moscow and Leningrad, but is better kept. From 1903 to 1921 it was the home of the Royal Naval College.

The inside is overpowering. Visitors see both the State Apartments and the Private Apartments used by Queen Victoria. If these do not seem very large it is perhaps because they are so prodigally overfurnished with masterpieces of sometimes hideous and sometimes affecting ingenuity. The Durbar Room, in elaborate plasterwork, was designed by John Lockwood Kipling, the poet's father, and the Indian decorative motives executed by Bhai Ram Singh. The Antler Room is fascinatingly ugly. All the rooms are heavy with portraits, including a fine Winterhalter of Maharajah Dhuleep Singh and a staggering collection of statues, pictures and glass cabinets: a wonderland for the connoisseur of Victoriana, a stuffed peacock for the modernist, and a magnet for charabancs.

The Swiss cottage, half a mile away in the grounds, is a chalet imported in 1853 as a playhouse for the Royal children, King Edward VII and his brothers and sisters. It has their model kitchen, their garden and special tools, and objects collected by and for them. More are in the Museum nearby, built in 1862: fossils, wonders from the Empire, beads and feathers, and a crocodile shot by the Duke of Connaught. There is an "Albert Barracks", a miniature fort which they built in 1860, and the Queen's bathing hut.

Part of Osborne is now a convalescent home for officers and civil servants.

Parkhurst [7]. *Parkhurst Forest* shrouds Parkhurst Prison, northwest of Newport, with its southern edge lying along the main road to Yarmouth. It is now about 11,000 acres, and the largest tract of woodland in the Island, administered by the Commissioner of Crown Lands. Once, as a Norman game forest, it was far more extensive and stretched to

OSBORNE HOUSE

OSBORNE: *The Swiss Cottage*

Newtown. As late as the reign of Charles II it was said that a squirrel might run on the tops of trees from Gurnard to Carisbrooke. The forest belonged to the Captain of the Island, with pasture rights for commoners. It is now pleasant thick woodland, with unusual wild flowers inside, and some light industry on the edge: not sinister, and the watch tower in the middle is for fire purposes, not for spotting escaped prisoners.

PARKHURST proper is a nexus of institutions on the main road just out of Newport, on the way north to Cowes. Busy, ugly, and developing fast, with houses Victorian, pre-fab, semi-detached or linear-brick modern, not now entirely for prison officers. It is an artificial intrusion into the Island, which, however, does not resent it as bitterly as might be imagined. It is rather proud of the prison, which has a very good security record. When prisoners *have* escaped, Islanders frequently left out food for them, a generation ago, with the windows of their houses left open. As well as the central prison is Camp Hill, a corrective training prison, and Albany Barracks. This, named after the Duke of York and Albany, long crumbled as a ghost memorial to the Napoleonic Wars, but, rebuilt, is to be incorporated in a new and model prison project.

On the east, facing the prison, is St Mary's Hospital, good contemporary institutional. The whole strip is hideous.

Porchfield [6]. This is a straggling village of a few old farms and cottages, a post-office and some modern brick houses, with a neat bridge over a brook that runs into the most eastern creek of Newtown estuary. It and *Locksgreen*, which is a continuation of it, are in good farmland in the otherwise largely uninhabited northern strip between the estuary and Gurnard, with Parkhurst Forest lying to the south. There are narrow lanes, and the underwood comes down to the edge of the Solent along both sides of Saltmead Ledge almost as though it is fringing an inland lake.

Quarr Abbey [3]. The ruins of the old Abbey of Our Lady of the Quarry lie visibly off the road from Newport to Ryde just before entering Binstead. There is now really only the usual enclosure wall of a Cistercian house to see, with ruins of some of the coast defences, and one of the fishponds. Yet the original abbey was the most important in the Island, and held extensive properties: the abbot was often Warden of the Island. It was founded as early as 1132 by Baldwin de Redvers, Lord of the Island, and built from the nearby quarries of Binstead. These also provided the stone for Winchester and Chichester cathedrals, and Winchester College. After the Dissolution of the Monasteries the property was bought about 1550, as a speculation of the brothers Mills, of Southampton, who sold much of the stone for the new castle defences at Cowes and Yarmouth. The site became farm property. The monks disappeared.

Four hundred years later they are back. The New Abbey lies at the end of a drive off the main road a mile from the ruins of the old, behind trees. Some Benedictine monks, exiled from Solesmes in France, came at the beginning of the century and settled first at Appuldurcombe. Seven years later they bought the land and started rebuilding at Quarr and had finished the new abbey by 1914. It achieved independence and its first Abbot in 1938. It is a very fine modern ecclesiastical building, designed by one of the community, Dom Paul Bellot. The quarry being exhausted, he used imported Flemish bricks of varying colours which combine into an

The Modern QUARR ABBEY, near Binstead

Chillerton Down, near Shorwell ☛

overall effect of rich peach, described as "rose-brick". The buildings incorporate a Victorian house, but the Abbey itself, finely vaulted and arched, with some dramatic use of brick patterns, is most effective. Being essentially a monastic oratory it has a tremendous choir and very short nave. It is rightly visited, but is essentially an active place of worship.

Rookley [13]. A busy strip of road where secondaries meet the main route from Newport to Godshill. Small farms, a general stores, characterless functional early 20th century houses, and a brickworks. It is in very nearly the geographical centre of the Island, and map names of farms and features around it – The Wilderness, Bleak Down, Bohemia, Bunker's Hill – suggest a remoteness which can still be felt, off the highway.

Ryde [8]. A modern resort, but still from the sea identifiable as the Victorian marine development of Brannon's steel-engravings, of 1840, when speculative building began. The town is well-set on a hillside still with plenty of trees, and the main streets slope up steeply from the front and the hotels to the spire of All Saints parish church, on the skyline. Ashley Down lies as a backcloth. In detail there are few buildings of individual interest – some round Lind Street and the Town Hall – and cheerful ugly ones above and below the Ryde Club in Spencer Road. *All Saints* in Queens Road is one of Sir Gilbert Scott's best churches, with a majestic 180 ft spire that dominates the view from the sea, and very rich alabaster pulpit, reredos and font. It was opened in 1867, rather downgrading St Thomas, built in 1827. The Roman Catholic church of St Mary's is a design by Hansom, who also designed the cab named

RYDE:
(above) *The Crown Hotel
in the High Street*
(below) *The Prince Consort*

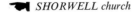 *SHORWELL church*

after him and Birmingham Town Hall. It is attractive inside. St James is embattled "Gothick" of 1829. The spire of Holy Trinity in Down Street shows up well, and there are other Victorian churches and chapels, some now derelict. These were the status symbols of the Victorian development of the fashionable resort from an eighteenth century fishing village amongst mudflats.

In 1826 the regular steam-packet between Ryde (or Ride) and Portsmouth was started. In 1824 the pier was finished, sand was replacing mud, and by the 'forties the hotels, boarding houses and shops were shooting up the hillside. The crenellated Ryde Castle, and the Royal Esplanade Hotel on the front still proudly witness the architecture of the Victorian prime. The Royal Squadron Hotel was indeed built in 1812, in time for Queen Victoria to stay with her mother as a girl, and again with her Consort whilst Osborne was being got ready. For Ryde was a modish resort, with its own yacht racing – the Royal Victorian Yacht Club had its foundation stone laid by the Prince Consort in 1846 – and many glories remain, with regattas particularly in July and August. But current prosperity is democratic, and Ryde is now essentially a base for day visitors from Portsmouth, with booking offices for scheduled trips round the Island by coach or by water. The front has gay Parade gardens, with canoe lake, pavilion and seasonal amenities, and seven miles of sand. The pier is nearly half a mile long, wide enough for pedestrians, trains and trams – horse trams till 1864, electric ones after 1880 (long before the London tubes) and now diesel. It is a functional pier of character, not just an amusement arcade on stilts into the sea.

Ryde became a borough in 1868 and now spreads ugly suburbs. But everywhere there are big Victorian and Edwardian houses with a certain dignity, usually prosperous guest houses. The population is about 20,000. This is doubled during the season, but

light industries and its importance as a local shopping centre keep Ryde alive in the months between the tourists, and a respectable home for, as the earlier guidebooks said with a proper sense, "many genteel families". Ryde is, indeed, both popular and provincially respectable.

St Catherine's [17]. *St Catherine's Down* is 781 ft high at its peak, six feet less than St Boniface, but the second highest in the Island. There is a car park at the top of the road from Blackgang up St Catherine's Hill, the easiest vantage point for views. A spot of pilgrimage is a small tower, *St Catherine's Offertory*, an old lighthouse. This Pharos was first set up by a Walter de Godeton, in 1328, as a penance for benefiting illegally from a wreck on the rocks below. It was kept by a priest who said Masses for travellers and trimmed the light. The light went out with the Reformation. In 1785, as wrecks continued, the Trinity Board started the other lighthouse, of which a stump remains, a few yards away, nearer the coast. It was quite ineffective, through misting, and this led to the erection of the new lighthouse below. The two ruins are popularly called, respectively, the Mustard Pot and the Pepper Box. On the Down a mile further north is the Alexandrian Pillar, visible for many miles. It is a 72 ft column with a ball on top, put up in 1814 to the Czar Alexander I of Russia, and later used, ironically, as a memorial to the British soldiers who fell in the Crimean War. There is also, for older, nameless dead, a tumulus.

ST CATHERINE'S LIGHTHOUSE is on the southern tip of the Island, on a flat strip resulting from some remote landslip, and looks white, warm and comfortable, being 136 ft above the sea and so undashed by waves. It was first used in 1840. It has six million candle power, a flashing light which reaches sixteen miles, and a distressing but invaluable foghorn. It is visited at the discretion of Trinity House, and there is literature about its technical efficiency.

St Helens [9]. The village stands on rising ground above Brading Harbour, round a delightful open green. Eighteenth century cottages with smuggling overtones and guest facilities, and a plaque on the house in Upper Green Road where lived the notorious Sophie Dawes. She was the daughter of a smuggler, graduated to the title of "The Queen of Chantilly" by becoming the mistress of the Duc de Bourbon. The church, rebuilt in 1830, lies isolated to the north, full of memorials to the former owners of the Priory – a mansion, once a Cluniac foundation. The old church stood on the shore – was ruinous by Elizabethan times – and is now represented only by its square tower, famous as a landmark. The "Holystones", pumicelike stones used for scouring ships' decks, were reputedly taken from its ruins. It is at the bottom of a pretty lane leading on to the golf course, reeds, wildfowl, a wharf, and a ferry across to Bembridge. Offshore lie the famous St Helen's Roads, the anchorage much mentioned in despatches by Nelson, and off the coast, here, too, brave Kempenfelt and his men were lost in the naval accident of 1782.

St Helens Common, inland, with gracious views, belongs to the National Trust.

St Lawrence [18]. An opulent village on the main coast road along the Undercliff: comfortable villas and modern bungalows in full sub-tropical luxuriance: cork trees, creepers and Italian gardens. The earlier cottages lead upwards to the tiny Norman "Old Church", which until 1842 was the smallest in England (25 ft. by 11 ft.). Then the Earl of Yarborough added 10 ft. to the chancel, a porch and a bell-tower. It is pretty and odd, if architecturally insignificant. A new church (1878) by Sir Gilbert Scott, is below on the main road, before a rash of development leading into Ventor. There is a little bathing beach at Woody Bay, and above on the downs is "High Hat" (455 ft.). *The Undercliff* is a geological freak some six miles long, and under half a mile wide, stretching between St

RYDE: Houses on the North side of Melville Street

Catherine's Point and Dunnose, to the east of Ventnor. It is a sheltered ledge formed by a series of landslips from the line of cliffs 200 ft. above. Sometimes a lower cliff exists on the seaward side, and sometimes it goes direct down to the water, thick with vegetation. The process has continued through history, and a specially heavy rainfall in 1928 cut the coast road between Blackgang and Ventnor north of St Catherine's Point, accounting for the modern road circling over the top of the cliff. Both sides of the road along the Undercliff are thickly wooded, often with strings of ivy among the roots and rocks, and the whole stretch is of great beauty, as well as of special interest to the geologist and botanist.

Sandown [14]. Unashamedly modern and prosperous, but so providently placed in fine coastal scenery, and rising so cheerfully from the bay that, despite having no architectural merit whatsoever it is easy to call it beautiful. Sandown, Lake and Shanklin are a continuous holiday strip looking out on to Sandown Bay, all enjoying a climate that invites round-the-year residence, and a summer that brings visitors in thousands. From the middle of the bay Culver Cliff lies away to the east, with the lower Red Cliff on this side of it, sloping to the development of Sandown. Then the cliff rises again to Shanklin, with its houses climbing above the sea, punctuated by spires: finally cliffs again, and foliage, round to Luccombe. From the inland, too, the approach is much the same for the whole strip, but less attractive: rather like coming in to Brighton from the Downs. Yet from the downs themselves the view is again superb – the neat roofs among the trees, and the pier pricking out into the bay with the mainland in the distance. And as yet virtually no disfiguring chim-

neys or disproportionate cement matchboxes.

Sandown does not appear at all on the early maps of Wight, and is the creation of the last hundred and fifty years. In Domesday it is just "Sande", and the property throughout most of history belonged to the Oglanders of Nunwell. The coast here needed defence, however, and Henry VIII built Sandham Castle as an important fort in 1541. When this was destroyed by the sea the Stuarts built another and there were successful actions against the French, and later against American privateers during the War of Independence. John Wilkes discovered the advantages of the place as a resort, and built Sandham Cottage as his "villa-kin". David Garrick and various literary-political figures of the late 18th century came to the Island as his guests and the story began. It went on with Darwin, Lewis Carroll, Hall Caine and the speculators.

The Esplanade is a mile of bars, cafes, bingo halls, fun fairs, hotels and boarding houses, behind a strong sea wall. When the tide is out there are excellent sands: the Pier is nearly a thousand feet long: the Pavilion seats nearly a thousand people: the Blue Lagoon is a roof terrace with a swimming pool. There is putting and a canoe lake. At the end of the Esplanade are the rockeries and lawns of the Battery Gardens, on the site of one old fort, and at the other end the Sandham Grounds, and a Zoo, on the site of another, but it is not yet Blackpool.

Behind the front is an unexceptional modern town with a general seaside flavour. Christ Church is a boom building of 1845. The Public Library has a famous collection of fossils, and behind the station is the road to the golf course and the waterworks. And to the lovely interior.

Seaview [9]. A synthetic name for a resort suburb of Ryde, two and a half miles away, and until recently shown on the map as "Seagrove Bay". The name aims at preserving the separate entity

officially lost by absorption in 1926. Firm sands, and a fine headland looking over the Solent, with wooded lanes behind, do indeed charm the same families back year after year. There are Seaview Mermaids, a special sort of yacht, and good prawn and lobster fishing. A modern little High Street, and St Peter's Church of 1861. There is a long stretch of cement toll road, stretching through to *Puckpool*, an old park now thirteen acres of marine facilities, and so on through to Ryde. The seawall walk at Seaview, hung between trees and water, is charming.

NETTLESTONE, now a southern inland tendril of Seaview, was a hamlet once in its own right, and does indeed have a church, and beautiful country lies behind it.

SPRING VALE, on the way to Puckpool, is little more than a terrace of houses, hotels, and sand-castles.

Shalfleet [6]. To the motorist a huddle of pretty red-roofed buildings and a church, overhung with trees, at a dip in the main road between Yarmouth and Newport. In reality it is quite a large parish, with a couple of hamlets and several outlying farms, stretching from the most forbidding part of the northern coast to the uplands of the central ridge of the Island. The church and the core of the village are above the stream, the Caul, which winds up from Calbourne into the Newtown estuary. Shalfleet itself means the "shallow creek". There is a fine farm facing the church, both on a rise above the thatched and tiled cottages. The church, one of the oldest in the Island, has a Norman tower with walls five feet thick, obviously defensive (the outside doorway is modern), presiding over a picture-book churchyard. The tower looks timeless, but in fact had a cupola added in 1754, and later a wooden steeple. These were removed, and the tower had subsequently to be underpinned, like Winchester, in 1912. A blurry tympanum on the north door is claimed to represent Daniel and two disparate lions (or David with

SHALFLEET: The five foot thick walls of the Norman Church tower

a lion and a bear): there are Purbeck marble pillars inside, and 13th century tracery, with some pleasant box pews. There are old roof timbers and a Jacobean pulpit. But there has been extensive restoration.

Some modern houses are decently screened by trees behind the church.

To the north lie heavily wooded areas full of primroses, reached by footpaths and unmade roads, to Bouldnor Cliff and Hamstead Ledge. These have through history slipped down into the Solent, helped at one time by the wash from the great liners beating the Blue Riband of the Atlantic. This left quicksands, gnarled tree trunks projecting from the sea, and some sense of desolation. Hamstead Grange is a modern house, and the excellent estate is still private, but Hamstead itself, once the home of John Pennethorne, brother of Sir James and also a pupil of Nash, is now destroyed. This area is now partly mottled with bungalows, and probably less adders abound than forty years ago, but much of it remains heavily wooded and rather bleak.

The Hamstead beds are amongst the most recent strata found in the Island, full of fossils, and rich quarry to the geologist.

NINGWOOD, to the south of Shalfleet, is a few cottages and farms set down a green leafy lane, and the Manor House is used as a Rest Home for Tired Horses.

Shanklin [14] is continuous, through Lake, with Sandown (q.v.) although technically they are two miles apart. They have almost the same population (7,000 each) but Shanklin is rather older, and with more pretension to elegance. The cliff here is a perpendicular wall a hundred and fifty feet high. The main part of the

(above) *SHANKLIN*

(below) *Keats Inn at SHANKLIN*

NEWPORT: A warehouse in Crocker Street

town – marine villas and Victorian private houses now usually hotels – lies at the top. Sloping roads at each end of the cliff lead down to the Esplanade, which can also be reached, more starkly, by electric lift. It has all the usual beach paraphernalia of eating and cavorting places, boating, bathing and a Summer Arcade. The pier, repaired from war-damage, has a casino and Dance Pavilion. Also a history – the Pluto pipe-line to Cherbourg, pumping petrol to the Allied Expeditionary Force during the 1939–45 war, started here. Above the Chalybeate Spring at the foot of the cliff are marine gardens, a Promenade and Shelter, and Keats Green. Keats wrote part of "Endymion" here, but found the place too expensive

SHANKLIN: Chine Lodge, Shanklin Chine

OLD SHANKLIN: Village

and moved to Carisbrooke, although he liked Shanklin for its climate and primroses. Now there are seas of hydrangeas.

The Chine is a particular tourist attraction. It is no longer the primaeval and forbidding torrent of the Romantics, but a narrow cleft in the soft greensand, winding down to the sea prettily between trees that meet overhead and slimy rock walls with green ferns. It is 180 ft. wide and nearly 300 ft. deep, with a path zigzagging down. A stream from the road at the top sometimes forms a cascade. It is commercialized, but attractive. The Rylstone Gardens, extending the whole southern length of the Chine, have lawns, conifers, evergreens and splendid sea views.

Shanklin Old Village looks like a film set, and is greatly admired. It has basically old cottages, dripping with roses and honeysuckle, and unnaturally perfect thatch. It has much Oxford lettering on the

tea shops, and a verse by Longfellow, with the English and American flags, on a drinking fountain. The old church, St Blasius, a hundred yards away, is magnificently placed beneath Shanklin Down, but architecturally unexciting. The Manor House is a holiday camp. The Crab Hotel is a magnet to many.

The best of Shanklin is the boarding houses and hotels of the peak period just over a hundred years ago, that line the front, and give the town its still remaining charm and character.

Shorwell [12]. Developed round the edges, and a traffic way, but perhaps the best village in the Island. It is two miles from Brighstone in the only opening in the range of downs from Gatcombe to Freshwater, with Brighstone Down (700 ft.) lying above the woods to the north, and the sea two miles to the south. Good thatched and stone cottages, well-

NEWCHURCH

grouped round the inn by the stream, and in glorious country, reached by a network of paths, well indicated.

The church (St Peter) is central: on a hill, with a square tower and weathervane added in 1617. The first church was built during the reign of Edward III, when the parishioners complained of having to take their dead five miles to burial, at Carisbrooke. The present building was made basically in 1440. It is an interesting church for antiquarians, although heavily restored, and has, like many Wight churches, a very competent guide-book. The 17th century pews all have 19th century poppy heads on them carved by Sir Henry Gordon, and there are brasses, a gun chamber, and a medieval stone pulpit (a rarity in Wight) with a Jacobean sounding-board. Also chained books and a large 15th century wall painting of St Christopher. Three naves and no chancel arch.

Shorwell was the village of three great houses, still extant:

NORTH COURT, hidden by trees half a mile above the church, was the home of the Leigh family and was begun by Sir John Leigh in 1615.

WEST COURT, on a corner just below the road to Brighstone, is early Tudor with later features: now a very attractive farm, beautifully kept. It belonged to the de Lisles.

WOLVERTON MANOR, south of West Court, is on the Yafford stream, and another mansion of the new men of the Jacobean period in the Island.

Thorley [5]. Quite a large inland parish of good farming land, just south-east of Yarmouth. The old church, betrayed by some overgrown yews facing the road, is now represented by remains of the porch, with a belfry, overgrown with brambles behind a fine farmhouse. This is on a corner coming from Yarmouth, and after crossing a tiny bridge over the disconsolate scar of the dismantled single-track railway line.

The rest of the houses, brick and stone, straggle along the main road, and form *Thorley Street*. The new Victorian church, St Swithin's, has a bell-cote and some intelligent use of red and yellow brick in the chancel. There are fine views from the rising ground to the south.

TOTLAND BAY: The pier

Totland [4] is Totland Bay, on the north-western tip of the Island, lying between Colwell Bay and Freshwater, and part of a continuous strip of holiday camps, bungalows and chalets. Totland means tootland, and a toot was a look-out. There used, in fact, to be a warning beacon on the headland. But otherwise the place has no history.

Although a resort it is largely residential, and in degree less overrun than the eastern places for day-trip visitors. It is in well-wooded country, with the downs above it, peppered with tumuli, and fine views across the West Solent to the mainland and Hurst Castle. An ugly brick structure in the foreground of the seascape from here and Colwell Bay is the Victorian Fort Albert, used recently for torpedo testing, and a further depot nearer Sconce Point is Fort Victoria.

Totland has a green suburban shopping centre, Broadway, a pocket pier and esplanade, and a pine wooded strip called the Turf Walk, with cliffs steepening towards Alum Bay on the west, the seaward face of Headon Hill. The church is a status symbol of 1875, to serve the newly-arriving villas. ALUM BAY was so-called from the alum mining for which a warrant was issued to Sir Richard Worsley in 1561, and remains as a natural wonder of variegated cliffs. The Bagshot sands emerge here from the land into the cliff face, and in the right light, and after rain, run down in perpendicular stripes of colour. There is also the depressing "blue slipper" fault of successive landslides. All this is happily exploited, and a long flight of wooden steps leads down the cliffs from the car park and the amenities, whilst shops sell ready-made test-tubes of the twelve distinct shades of coloured sand for those too lazy to collect their own. It is a key spot for the coach tours round the Island, always busy. When it was wild, and the cliffs

really were reached by a steep and rugged chasm, on unmade paths, the sudden revelation of cliffs shot like silk, beneath the gorse above, with the sea below and the white Needles beyond, must have been even more remarkable. On top of the cliff is a memorial to mark the fact that Marconi made his first experimental wireless transmissions from here, fathering the masts which now peak some of the higher downs.

Away to the extreme west the *Needles* themselves jag out into the sea, photographed and over-familiar from every angle. There are five of them (of which only three are conspicuous) – isolated chalk spires, much larger and more impressive from the sea than from the land. A fourth, Lot's Wife, which was 120 ft. high, and the only one like a needle, fell on a calm day in 1764, with a crash that is supposed to have been heard on the mainland. An arch

joining the final rock to the mainland fell about the time of Waterloo. They are the jagged end of the ridge of hills which runs across the Island, and jut out, with a lighthouse at the end and a coastguard station above, to welcome and warn the ships from the western ocean. The lighthouse, built in 1858, is 80 ft. high, but dwarfed by the cliffs. Its light is visible for 15 miles, and it has a powerful and mournful foghorn.

To their south is Scratchell's Bay, and the beach stretching to below Tennyson Down.

Ventnor [18]. A watering place rather than a resort, and more dignified than Sandown or Shanklin. It is also older – indeed after Ryde it is the oldest of the 19th century watering places, and modernization has not spoilt the effect. The front may be garish in detail, but the town, facing due south, still climbs from the sea as

VENTNOR: The station, now disused

THE NEEDLES from an old engraving showing "Lot's Wife" which fell in 1764.

delightfully as in the early prints, and the superb, almost sub-tropical climate remains, plugged endlessly but justifiably.

It was the discovery of the climate which created Ventnor, which in 1830 was a mill, an inn, and a few fishermen's cottages, part of the parish of Bonchurch. Sir James Clarke in 1829 wrote a popular medical treatise on "The Influence of the Climate in the Prevention and Cure of Organic Diseases", citing the Undercliff as good for pulmonary disorders, and the speculators moved in. Soon there were lodging houses, villas, a church and a mock medieval castle (recently destroyed). Town Commissioners, appointed annually, were created by Act of Parliament in 1846, and soon provided power, drainage, an Esplanade and sea-wall, and an early attempt at planning. Ventnor has flourished ever since. The Esplanade is short, but has a pier, a canoe-lake and all the foreshore trappings. Above is a Winter Garden, 1937 glass-fronted, with a cascade, and everywhere are sun-lounges, shelters and "attractions". Also seats, which are necessary, for the town climbs sharply up from the sea in three tiers, with roads zig-zagging to the skyline. There is a florid little Town Hall Theatre of 1878, but few individual buildings are of interest, and they tend to get newer as they climb upward. More easily from the sea than from on land the Victorian marine villas and the balconied hotels of the early development stand out, often framed by palms and other exotics. It is pardonable

to compare it rather with the Riviera than the English south coast.

Wellow [5] is a hamlet on the road between Thorley Street and Newbridge. It has an inn, a few old houses and some bungalows, with fine wooded country to the north, fine rolling farm uplands to the south, and Yarmouth church tower showing over the trees to the north-west.

Whippingham [2]. This is an extensive parish between Wootton Creek and the Medina, but with virtually no houses except a post-office, expensive and ornate Victorian almshouses, and the church. It was the Royal Church for Osborne, down the road, and is another temple of Victoriana. The original church was one of those mentioned in Domesday, but Nash, who was moving in to nearby East Cowes Castle, completely restored this in 1795. In 1860 the Prince Consort again rebuilt on the site what we see today. It was to his own design – a romantic Teutonic adaptation of Early English. It is basically a Latin cross, with a long chancel for the Osborne pews. The dumpy building has a tower with five pinnacles, one at each corner and a larger one in the middle, and there is an Indian teak lych-gate. It remains an architectural freak, but not to be despised.

Inside is a marble reredos given by Edward VII, a heartbroken monument to the Prince Consort erected by Queen Victoria, a lavish Battenberg Chapel, and numerous other royal memorials.

Retainers of all degree are buried in the churchyard, among cypresses.

Whitwell [17]. A pleasant unselfconscious inland village. It has a long main street, with ordinary unremarkable houses, and seems not affected by the show village of Godshill, three miles north, or St Lawrence and its lush development, two miles south. The church, well-placed on a corner, has a good 16th century tower, with an odd south pillar to the chancel arch, with a capital larger than its column.

Wroxall [14]. A large inland village behind Ventnor, a good take-off for St Martins Down and the best approach to Appuldurcombe House (q.v.) which lies off it to the west. Plain modern and Victorian houses, with new development towards Ventnor and a large and conspicuous cemetery to the north. St John's is a plain little Victorian church with pinewood pews and a tower added without distinction in 1911. It is an unassuming place, full of guest houses and with a caravan site, but not suggesting undue exploitation.

Wootton [8] ("Wood-town") Creek is a beautiful tidal inlet surrounded by copsewood and the ancillaries of yachting. The village houses are almost all modern, and bungalows lead off the main road from Cowes to the church (St Edmund). This has a Norman doorway and a Jacobean pulpit, but is chiefly remarkable for its connections with the Lisle family.

WHIPPINGHAM: The Almshouses

WHIPPINGHAM: Church designed by the Prince Consort and A. J. Humbert

Sir John Lisle, unlike most of the Island gentry of the Civil War period, was an ardent Parliamentarian.

WOOTTON BRIDGE is a modern village which has formed along the main road to Ryde, at the point where the creek ceases to be tidal. There is an inn, a small quay, quite gay with boats, but new houses without any distinction, below a few villas hidden among the trees.

Yarmouth [5]. A pleasant little port with some history. It was Eremue in Domesday Book, received a charter in 1135, was briefly the headquarters of King John in 1206, and sent two members to Parliament from 1304 till 1832. It was often the seat of the Governor of the Island. It fills and empties all day as visitors pour off the ferries and scatter across the Island. From the sea it appears to be just a small quay, with a harbour to its west, a stone fort in the middle, an odd crenellated house with gun-ports in the sea-wall, a pier, and some scattered roofs dominated by a church with a disproportionate tower. This is in fact about all it is, but it retains character. Yachtsmen stay there, and there are guest

houses and two good hotels, but it is not overrun by visitors. It is the capital of West Wight, and a good centre from which to see the whole Island, or to stay and watch the traffic up and down the Solent.

The quay, mildly continental ("Gentlemen, Messieurs, Herren") is primarily for the motor ferries from Lymington (successors to the paddle steamers of 1830 and the golden age), and the newly dredged harbour is usually crowded. A breakwater on the seaward side is visited by cormorants, known here as "Isle of Wight parsons". On the landward side is the Embankment of 1836, with a drawbridge over the Yar connecting with the Freshwater peninsula, and low-lying river banks and saltings behind.

One side of the landing-stage is framed by the castle, built after

YARMOUTH:

◀ *The Tide Mill*

The harbour

Cowes and Sandown Castles by Henry VIII in 1547, and afterwards modified by various Captains of the Island. It is really a large rectangular gun-emplacement, with living accommodation behind for the garrison. This, bored, was removed in 1885 and the castle is now spotlessly Ministry of Works, who provide an excellent guide for those architecturally and historically interested. (It has the first arrow-head bastion in England). Part of the back premises are now incorporated in the George Hotel, which has high panelled rooms, in one of which Charles II was the guest of Sir Robert Holmes, who lived here as Governor.

Another Holmes, Lord Thomas, appears in the inscription on the little Town Hall in Pier Place, almost next door, which he rebuilt in 1765. It is a pretty little square brick building, used as a meat market till 1888, and now with the charters and history on show upstairs. But the most visible evidence of the powerful Holmes tradition is the life-size statue of Sir Robert himself in the little chapel of the church, now used as a vestry. He was a soldier of fortune knighted for exceptional services in Africa, America and the Baltic, and Captain of the Wight from 1662 to 1692. He captured a Dutch vessel off the Guinea coast with the gold from which the first guineas were made, and in 1664 he took New Amsterdam, thenceforward called New York. The statue is rather ridiculous, with too big a head, substantiating the anecdote that it was really an unfinished one of Louis XIV. Holmes captured the French ship that was taking it to Paris, and made the artist substitute his own features for those of the king. It looks like it. The church itself (St James) was built after 1614, nothing but ruins then remaining of an earlier one burnt in successive raids by the French. Inside it is darkly restored and the upper stage of the tower was added unnecessarily in 1831.

The Pier is 700 ft. long and has a waiting-room with a collection of photographs of eminent Victorians by Thackeray's friend, and Tennyson's, Margaret Cameron. This is much prized by historians of

photography and ignored by visitors. On the opposite side of the pier from the castle is the Royal Solent Yacht Clubhouse, with its own jetty, and there are other private jetties stretching to a pleasant green common on the edge of the town. Above the middle of all this is the crenellated house with the mock gun-ports, faithfully repainted since a David Urry RN, a many-times mayor and worthy, put them there to hoax the French in the 18th century. There are a few shops, including a good bookseller, a few Victorian houses, more Edwardian ones, newer suburbs and a pleasant old brick Mill overlooking the river. But Yarmouth, apart from the escape to Newport, is almost an island, and cannot sprawl. It looks compact and attractive, from the downs above Thorley. It remains cheerful and faintly tarry, more fish than chips.

Yaverland [15]. A small village in a fold of the southern slope of Bembridge Down. It is now also an inland extension of Sandown Promenade, which suddenly becomes a peaceful country street of old cottages here, leading to the usual pattern of church and manor house. The church, almost touching the manor, and dwarfed by it, may indeed have originally been its chapel. There is a Norman doorway inside a modern porch, and much of the church dates from the 12th century, but it was all heavily restored in 1888. The manor belonged to the Russells who founded the noble house of Bedford, and Sir Theobald Russell of Yaverland died within sight of his home here defending the East Medina from the French in 1340. Two early manor houses were indeed burned down by the invaders, and the present one is good Jacobean, with a gabled front.

EAST COWES Castle by John Nash, demolished 1965

The pier at YARMOUTH

NINETEENTH CENTURY CHURCHES

THE nineteenth-century development of the Island naturally led to a great deal of church building. The Chapel of St Thomas, Ryde, was rebuilt by John Sanderson in 1827, and the much more interesting St James's, a proprietary chapel, dates from the same year. Holy Trinity, Cowes, 1831–2, was designed by Benjamin Bramble of Portsmouth.

St Catherine's, Ventnor, 1836–7, was designed by Robert Ebbels, the architect of a good many cheap churches, in the Midlands and elsewhere. The Holy Spirit, Newtown, an elegant and imposing little chapel, E.E., with a plaster vault, was built in 1837 from plans by A. F. Livesay. St John's, Newport, also 1837, is only remarkable for the monument by J. S. Westmacott to the Rev. William Carus Wilson, editor of *The Friendly Visitor* and *The Children's Friend*, who appears as Mr Brocklehurst in *Jane Eyre*.

Thomas Hellyer of Ryde was responsible for the slim E.E. churches of Holy Trinity, Ryde, 1841–5, and St John's, Oakfield, 1843: in 1844 he rebuilt most of Binstead. St Paul's, Barton, is a very pleasant Norman church, 1845, by J. W. Wild, an architect who believed that churches should be simple and solemn in style, and was not a Gothic revivalist. Christchurch, Sandown, by J. Woodman of Shanklin, was consecrated in 1847: it has been much enlarged since. In the new church of Bonchurch, 1847–8, Benjamin Ferrey used the Norman style, as he quite often did.

S. W. Daukes, who was interested in railways as well as churches, was chosen as the architect of the new St Thomas's, Newport, which was begun in 1854, and consecrated early in 1857: it is a church that looks as though it has been transported from London.

Whippingham, probably the most visited church in the Island, was rebuilt by A. J. Humbert, the architect of Sandringham, in consultation with the Prince Consort. The style is Rhenish Gothic: the chancel, which was built first, is more Gothic than the nave and transepts.

Hellyer designed Seaview, 1861–4, which was considered to be twenty years behind the times. Holy Trinity, Ventnor, is a very good Victorian church, with some fittings that are later, but in keeping: the architect was C. E. Giles, and the date was 1860–2. St Michael's, Swanmore, Ryde, was designed by the Rev. W. Gray, an amateur, who had acted as diocesan architect to Newfoundland: the local architect R. J. Jones superintended the work. Its exterior is French Gothic at its most functional: inside, the nave has a polychrome brick lining, and the vaulted chancel looks something like the work of Burges. It was partly built in 1862, and completed later. R. J. Jones also rebuilt the church of Brooke, which was burned in 1863.

Arthur Cates rebuilt St Mary's, West Cowes, in 1867: Nash's tower of 1816, which is also a vault for himself and his family, was to have been remodelled, but was fortunately left alone. Hellyer designed St Saviour's, Shanklin, 1868–9, and recast East Cowes in 1868–70.

Sir Gilbert Scott contributed the handsome church of All Saints', Ryde, which was begun in 1869, consecrated in 1872, and finished ten years later. His new church at St Lawrence, 1876–8, is rather ordinary.

C. L. Luck designed two simple and quite satisfactory churches— St Paul's, Shanklin, and St John's, Sandown, consecrated in 1876 and 1881.

The Good Shepherd, Lake, 1892, was designed by Temple Moore, who was always good. Gurnard, 1892–3, by E. P. Loftus Brock, makes a disappointing ending to the century.

B. F. L. CLARKE

SHANKLIN: St Saviour's Church

INDEX

*An asterisk indicates an entry under its own name in the gazetteer

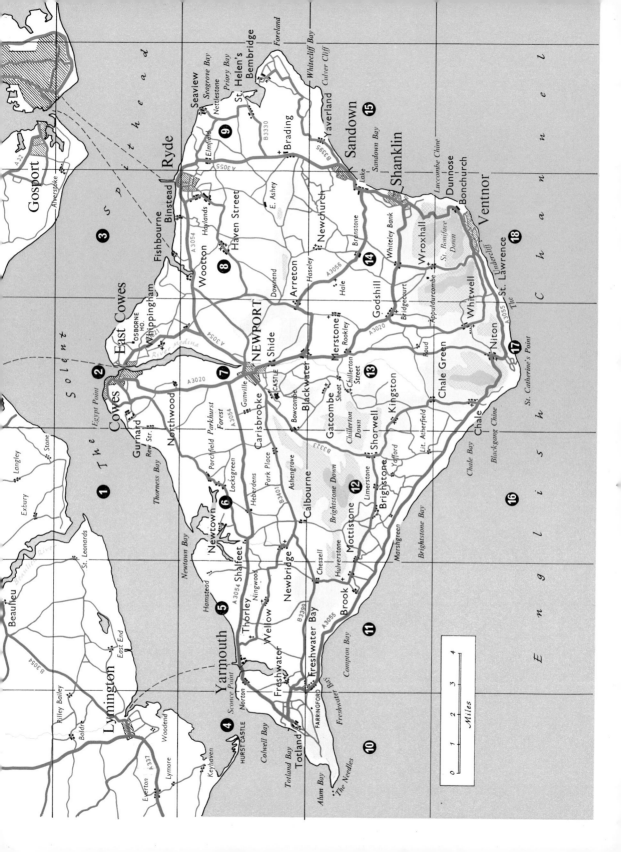